Psychological Aesthetics

Psychological Aesthetics

Painting, Feeling and Making Sense

David Maclagan

Jessica Kingsley Publishers
London and Philadelphia

First published in the United Kingdom in 2001
by Jessica Kingsley Publishers
116 Pentonville Road
London N1 9JB, UK
and
400 Market Street, Suite 400
Philadelphia, PA 19106, USA

www.jkp.com

Library of Congress Cataloging in Publication Data
Maclagan, David, 1940–
    Psychological aesthetics : painting, feeling, and making sense / David Maclagan.
        p. cm
    Includes bibliographical references and index.
    ISBN 1-85302-834-7 (pb : alk paper)
        1. Aesthetics--Psychological aspects. 2. Art therapy. I. Title.

    BH301.P78 M33 1999
    701'..15 21--21

                                                                99-041644

British Library Cataloguing in Publication Data
Maclagan, David
    Psychological aesthetics : painting, feeling and making sense
    1.Aesthetics 2.Art therapy 3.Psychoanalysis and art
    I.Title
    616. 8'91656

    ISBN 1853028347

                    ISBN-13: 978 1 85302 834 2
                    ISBN-10: 1 85302 834 7

Contents

Acknowledgements

In some ways this book has been written from a position of isolation; not just in terms of having to redefine what might be meant by 'aesthetic' and 'psychological' against the grain of current preconceptions, but also in the sense that the constituency I am appealing to seems as yet barely visible. I caught glimpses of it in the work of the London Convivium for Archetypal Studies, begun by Noel Cobb and the late Eva Loewe, with its passionate insistence on the links between art, beauty and soul-making; but sometimes this felt too elegant, too well composed. I knew that I was looking for something else; something inarticulate and anarchic that also refused the all-embracing edicts of psychoanalysis. The benefit of this is perhaps a degree of independence from any particular school of thought; the drawback, that some of my own ideas may seem a bit too speculative or unformed.

However, a glance at the contents will show that certain writers have been sources of excitement and challenge to me: Anton Ehrenzweig, James Hillman (in person as well as on the page), Jean-François Lyotard and Maurice Merleau-Ponty. I would also like to salute a recently recognised kindred spirit, James Elkins.

Much of the material in this book derives from teaching the MA in Art and Psychotherapy at the Centre for Psychotherapeutic Studies, University of Sheffield. I am grateful to John Henzell, my collaborator on this course, and above all to the students who over half a dozen years encouraged me and helped me further my thinking before the course was closed down. I also owe a debt to Linney Wix and the art therapy students at the University of New Mexico, who invited me over to talk about psychological aesthetics in 1996. I have also learned a great deal from the patients I worked with earlier as an art therapist in Broomhills therapeutic community.

Other friends and colleagues who have encouraged me or helped me in my thinking, sometimes without knowing it, include: Iain Biggs, Neil Bolton, Peter Byrne, Roger Cardinal, Clayton Eshleman, Angela Heskett, Sean Homer, Howard McGoneghy, Michael Edwards, Michael Ginsborg, Simon Lewty, Stephen Newton, Michael Podro, Geneviève Roulin, Rita Simon and Michel Thévoz. Clayton Eshleman and Gregory Corso also need to be thanked for their kind permission to reproduce their copyright material.

Last, but most important of all, I would like to acknowledge how much I have been formed and nourished by the experience of painting, both as an artist in my own studio, as a workshop leader and as a visitor to all kinds of museums, galleries, exhibitions and studios. In a very real sense painting has kept me alive.

The publishers acknowledge permission to quote from the following copyright source:

'The Circle of Styles', by Rita Simon, reproduced on p.94, from *The Symbolism of Style: Art as Therapy* (Routledge, 1992). Reproduced by kind permission of the Author and Routledge, London.

Introduction

What does 'psychological aesthetics' mean? Although the term may be unfamiliar, it refers to the relation between the actual (aesthetic) qualities of painting, such as line, colour, handling, composition and so on and the inner (psychological) effects that these have on the spectator. 'Aesthetic' in this sense is grounded in the material properties of painting, rather than referring to some disembodied realm of judgements about beauty or truth. 'Psychological' also refers to a somewhat different range of experience from the traditional psychology of perception. Here it suggests the complex and shifting array of sensations, feelings, fantasies, thoughts and other less easily categorisable events of mental life that accompany all our perceptions, whether we are aware of them or not. This is something that could be called the 'psychological lining of experience'.

Such reverberations are in evidence wherever art reproduces some life event or situation of human interest, most obviously in the narratives of literature, drama or film. But it is also present even in passages of apparently inert description, and this is especially true for painting. Certain landscapes or still lives, even though they seem to have the same immediacy and transparency as language, still offer a source of pleasure in the visual illusion they provide. Even the most factual or impassive of such representations still carries a psychological lining: the scrupulous, glassy neutrality of a Saenredam interior or a Canaletto view, for example, conveys a certain cool detachment and 'objectivity' which has its own psychological nuances.

Hence, no matter how realistic a painting is or how impressive its subject-matter, it is never simply a souvenir or recreation of the original moments when this psychological lining of experience was felt: it translates and intensifies them in its own particular ways. These depend crucially on the aesthetic qualities of painting mentioned above. For example, Van Gogh wrote in a letter about the sky of his 'Sower' (1888) as follows: 'The sky chrome yellow, almost as bright as the sun itself, which is chrome yellow 1 with a little white, while the rest of the sky is chrome yellow 1 and 2 mixed. Thus very yellow.' In the same letter he goes on to say: 'There are many touches of yellow in the soil, neutral tones produced by mixing purple with the yellow, but I couldn't care less what the colours are in reality' (quoted Gayford and Wright 1999, p.380).

The psychological lining of experience is not only altered by its material translation into paint: the actual aesthetic features of a painting – such as its pressure of line, density of colour, coherence or incoherence of form – have their own independent psychological contribution to make.

Psychological aesthetics is the field in which what we study are the interactions between painting at the level of 'facture' (handling) and the 'feeling' or making sense that it prompts in us. However, this interaction is not as simple as it is sometimes made out to be: the traffic between a painting and the spectator is not one-way. Conventional assumptions about communication or expression in art assume that a painting transmits an already established message to us and that we register this more or less successfully. But perception always involves a complex interaction between viewers and what they 'see', and our experience of paintings enhances such reactions. In fact paintings can be said to function as 'condensers' of such interactions.

A still-life by Bonnard, for example, can play them back to us in slow motion by inviting (or sometimes forcing) us to try and accommodate the discrepancies between the familiarity of its subject and the actual passages of paint that refuse to correspond in a straightforward way to its details. This illegibility may only appear on closer inspection, when we begin to notice all kinds of crazy local adventures in Bonnard's use of line and colour. To some extent these echo, or evoke, a correspondingly delicious uncertainty about our perception of equivalent scenes in real life.

Even in the case of more comfortably representational works, there is an alternation between 'seeing through' a painting, to what it represents, and making the painting itself the focus of our attention.[1] Painting that draws attention to its 'facture' or material handling, dramatises its aesthetic effects, and certain kinds of abstract painting, such as Abstract Expressionism, might be said to do this exclusively. These exchanges between spectators and the painting they are feeling their way into often take place at a largely unconscious level: we may register various effects without being aware of how we came to experience them. This subliminal dimension of aesthetic experience is something larger and more diffuse than what is usually understood by 'unconscious' in its psychoanalytic sense (as we shall see in Chapter Two). To try to explore this domain, to tune in to its complexities and to grapple with the difficulties of 'making sense', is to be engaged in what I shall call the 'creative reception' of painting, as opposed to a more passive assimilation or enjoyment of it.[2] It should be clear by now why such creative reception has to be intimately involved with psychological aesthetics.

Mention of the word 'aesthetic' conjures up, however, all sorts of prejudices and resistances and taps into a widespread suspicion of the term. It is a word that has acquired notoriously abstract and sophisticated connotations; it is associated with philosophical or critical debates that often seem rarified or pedantic. In the history of aesthetics, from Plato onward, the value and purpose of art depended upon its relation to beauty and to truth. This relation was often problematic: the very sorts of aesthetic qualities upon which I shall be concentrating in this book were suspect precisely on account of their close involvement with matter and the senses.

To make matters more difficult, beauty itself has, in the history of art since the Renaissance, been progressively re-visioned. There has been an increasingly contradictory relationship between conventional norms of beauty and works of art that seek to challenge or refuse them. In Mannerism, for example, established styles of representation and expression were deliberately distorted or exaggerated.

By the mid-nineteenth century notions of beauty in art were effectively divided between academic and sentimental stereotypes and a more original or avant-garde art in which a degree of strangeness or even shock was a necessary ingredient for true beauty. The history of the word 'bizarre' is instructive with regard to this. In the early Renaissance 'bizarre' was associated with senseless madness; later it came to denote the eccentric, and eventually it became a quintessential sign of creativity. By the 1850s it had acquired a crucial aesthetic status. Baudelaire, for example, claimed that:

> The beautiful is always bizarre.[...] Now how could this bizarreness – necessary, irreducible, infinitely varied, and determined by milieu, climate, custom, race, religion and the artist's temperament – ever be controlled by the Utopian rules that are conceived in some ordinary little scientific temple on this planet, without mortal danger to art itself? (quoted Gilman 1988, p.241)

It is only a few steps from this cult of the bizarre to more extreme or even perverse forms of beauty which are bound to have pathological undertones.

The 'aesthetic' effects of art have in effect come to be increasingly separable from any moral purpose they might be supposed to have. Instead, these effects can be said to belong to a realm which is as much one of 'feeling', in both its emotional and its sensuous forms, as of truth or propriety. This new territory of aesthetic experience touches on strange and extreme forms of human psychological experience, often outside the norm.

Indeed, in the more provocative forms of so-called 'decadent' art it seems as if artists are deliberately flouting the conventions that link aesthetic attraction and moral effect (a recent, equally deliberate, reversal of this can be seen in

Robert Mapplethorpe's erotic photographs). Actually, fin de siècle decadence leads a double life. As a quasi-scientific term it was key in the theories of psycho-social degeneration exemplified by the works of Max Nordau and Cesare Lombroso and was used to account for the supposed links between nervous instability and artistic lifestyle. Later on it was still being invoked in the Nazi 'Entartete Kunst' exhibitions of 1933 and after, where 'unhealthy' art was portrayed as having a deleterious effect on the body of society.

But these 'scientific' theories and images of decadence simultaneously enjoyed a kind of underground or black market value, where artists deliberately cultivated the very features that were being disapproved of (much as sixteenth century artists cultivated the attributes of the melancholic temperament). This meant not only an uninhibited attitude towards such 'psychopathological' features of life as masturbation, suicide or immorality – all of which feature in the works of Expressionist artists – but a parallel defiance of bourgeois standards of artistic decorum and good taste. Rimbaud's famous boast 'I sat Beauty on my knee and found her tart. And I insulted her' ('Une Saison en Enfer', my translation) sums up the mixture of ennui and aggression that often coloured decadent aesthetics.[3]

So while aesthetic qualities were sometimes thought of as being utterly detached from anything mundane or ordinary, and from any purpose, practical or moral, they were also associated with extreme psychological states, whether of ecstasy or depravity. No wonder that in other quarters 'aesthetic' was used in a pejorative sense, to refer to whatever was most irrelevant and self-indulgent about the art world.

Yet aesthetic experience is, in its etymology ('breathing in') a far more fundamental and inescapable aspect of experience. As one recent writer put it: 'To the extent that every thing, every place, every event is experienced by an aware body with sensory directness and immediate significance, it has an aesthetic element' (Berleant 1990). This fundamental level of aesthetic experience is, of course, something that can be built on and cultivated through further experience. This 'cultivation' is not just a matter of the gradually acquired appreciation of artworks; it also enters into the world of our imagination, or what psychoanalysis calls phantasy life: 'Aesthetic knowledge is decisive to our ability to represent the world to ourselves, that is, form a phantasy life with which to imagine and think' (Likierman 1989, p.134). As we shall see, it is not just experiences of nature, but our capacity to inhabit works of art imaginatively that contribute to the richness and depth of phantasy life.

Aesthetics is often assumed to be concerned with judgements of beauty or ugliness, but it actually taps into a much wider range of response. This includes not only such qualities as the awkward, the garish, the bizarre or the kitsch, but even the apparent absence of any quality, as in the dull or the indifferent. In this respect aesthetic response is like physical taste: it is not just the sweet or savoury that count, but also the flat, the bland or the dead. As James Hillman (1998) points out, it is not so much ugliness that is the opposite of aesthetic as an-aesthesia (I shall return to this in Chapter Five).

Another common assumption about aesthetic experience, and the judgements that are associated with it, is that it is largely informed by personal prejudices and subjective preference; so much so that there is no real criterion for discriminating between one opinion and another. It is true that the combination of psychological and aesthetic response with which we are here concerned has an undeniable 'inner' dimension; but that does not mean that it is to be dismissed as 'subjective' and therefore invalid. As one philosopher has recently reminded us in this context: 'There are indeed truths which may be subjectively experienced, but that these truths only emerge in subjective consciousness does not render them subjective' (Davey 1999, p.16). The fact that aesthetic experience engages with works of art that have an independent existence gives it an anchor in external reality. Of course, this 'existence' is itself the product of the spectator's creative encounter (as we shall see in Chapter Two), but it makes a crucial difference. A painting can then become the arena for an exchange between the supposedly subjective dimension of the spectator's experience and the work's actual external features. This exchange is a reciprocal one, in which each is modified by the other.

Looking at certain paintings provides some concrete examples of this. Each painting in Joseph Albers' series 'Homage to the Square' has the same composition of three squares of subtly different colour nesting inside one another like Chinese boxes. To begin with these squares appear quite distinct; but as your eye relaxes into the painting as a whole their colour begins to lift off and melt into a kind of nameless colour-film that floats over the painting's surface, so that its very substantiality seems to evaporate.[4]

Similar effects can be experienced with some of Rothko's late canvases (such as the 'chapel' currently in London's Tate Modern) or with some of Bridget Riley's so-called 'Op Art' paintings. These effects are not, however, purely optical: they are not simply illusions that are the result of certain perceptual 'mechanisms'. They depend upon a collaborative response from the viewer, a willingness to 'enter into' the painting. Such examples show the more dramatic tip of what is a vast iceberg of other aesthetic effects, many of which are extremely fragile, and for that reason vulnerable to a careless or inconsiderate way of looking. In this respect painting is usually a more vulnerable art form than, say, music or film. Nor are these effects purely 'visual': they are, as I have suggested, inextricably bound up with psychological responses, even if we may not at first be aware of them. If we accept that there is a psychological lining to experience, and if painting has its own particular ways of rehearsing this, then it might seem that this would above all involve the world of emotions or of feeling.

However 'feeling' is rather more complicated than this. The word is both a noun and a verb, referring to processes of sensation or exploration, as well as to emotion as one possible result of such processes. We do not in fact always know which comes first, the perception or sensation, or the emotional response. Academic psychology may find it convenient to assume that one is stimulus and the other response; but it is often hard to tell whether a particular feeling makes us tune into a specific sense impression, or whether the latter somehow prompts the former. There may be an elusive truth embodied in the fact that the word 'feeling' refers to both a process and to its result.

Even at the level of sensation, feeling turns out to have a hybrid nature: as the phenomenologist Merleau-Ponty (1964) wrote: 'There is a circle of toucher and touched, the touched grasps the toucher; there is a circle of the visible and the seer, the seer is not outside visible existence; there is even an inscription of touching in the visible, of seeing in the tangible, and vice versa...' (p.188, my translation).

Perhaps 'feeling' has blurred edges at both the perceptual and the emotional level. There are sometimes feelings that it is impossible to situate one side or the other of this categorial divide: they are also most likely to be feelings that are difficult or impossible to put into words. It may well be that painting has a particular involvement with precisely these non-verbal or pre-verbal 'feelings'.

The phrase 'making sense' also occurs in the title of this book. 'Sense' as a verb has a degree of overlap with 'feeling': it has undertones both of an indirect or intuitive way of being in touch with feelings ('I sensed his fear') as well as of more rational constructions and the meanings they engender ('This makes no sense'). Making sense of a painting may sound at first like an interpretative or analytic business, an attempt to specify and articulate its content, presumably in words. This impression may be borne out by much of the art historical and art critical writing we encounter; but in practice making sense of paintings is not such a strictly rational enterprise. What is actually involved may be a mixture of intellectual understanding and imagination, of focused or articulate with informal or inarticulate forms of understanding.

If this is so, then psychoanalysis, with its involvement with the threshold between conscious and unconscious levels of experience, might seem to offer an appropriate way of making sense of painting, all the more so when the various images of unpredictability and inspiration traditionally associated with the artist are taken into account. It has certainly come to occupy an authoritative position in relation to those meanings of a painting which lie beneath its surface and run counter to its consciously intended ones, and are thus 'unconscious' in a dynamic sense.

Part of the attraction of psychoanalytic interpretation is that it has its own devious form of logic, yet is at the same time beyond normal standards of proof. By conjuring up the mirage of an alternative 'unconscious' intentionality which is in competition with consciousness, psychoanalysis (at least in its classical, Freudian forms) sets up modes of explaining a painting's hidden meaning that in effect act out a rivalry with the creative work they are purporting to analyse. Unfortunately, as we shall see in Chapter One, the psychoanalytic privileging of depth over surface also has the effect of splitting the 'superficial' aesthetic level of a painting from its 'deep' unconscious meaning, so that the aesthetic and the psychological are divorced from one another.

As we shall see, not every meaning that can be found in a painting as the result of expanding our creative response to it has to be called 'unconscious' in this sense. However, the popularisation of psychoanalysis and the extension of its influence far beyond the consulting room has reached the point where its concepts of unconscious meaning have become almost synomymous with the 'psychological' significance of works of art. Many people thus fight shy of exploring the psychological aspects of an artist's work because they feel this would be trespassing on psychoanalytic territory.

The psychoanalytic assumption that a work of art's 'unconscious' content is in conflict with the artist's conscious aims and intentions, and has therefore been repressed, makes it difficult for us to imagine a psychological lining to our experience that might be unconscious in more subliminal ways. But our psycho aesthetic responses to painting can open out new avenues into what could be called the preliminary life of the mind. Making sense of these, instead of invoking an a priori unconscious content, would be a more experimental or creative process, and one that might shed light on a broader range of the psychological than psychoanalysis does, as we shall see in Chapter Three.

At its best, psychoanalytic writing about painting does convey the sense of an exploration that is provisional or inconclusive. A style of writing about art that tries to pin sense down or to arrive at definitive conclusions usually has too programmatic or authoritarian a flavour to it, and may even feel as if it is doing some kind of violence to its subject. But not all writing about aesthetic experience or its psychological resonance has to be so strictly analytic. If psychoanalytic writing about art sometimes parallels the creative impetus of the works it focusses on, then other forms of creative reception can have a comparable kinship with the open-ended nature of much painting.

There has been much talk recently about the 'death of painting', yet in many ways the life of painting still remains to be explored. This 'life' is not simply inherent in the material energy of the painting itself – in the career of its lines, the weight of its brushmarks or the temperature of its colour, for example – but is also inherent in a painting's independent existence. True, this may be subject to change – pigments may fade or self-destruct, supports disintegrate – but there is a real sense in which most paintings outlive the original circumstances in which they were first created.

This survival is not just a literal one, but a symbolic and cultural one, in that the work continues to be the object of renewed attention, and its meanings consequently alter and expand. Its independence is thus as much psychological as physical: its significance, even if it was initially closely tethered to the individual circumstances of the artist who created it, gradually becomes more collective, less personal. Its aesthetic and psychological life is centrifugal: as one writer recently put it: 'Aesthetic experience is the occasion of an artwork commencing and recommencing its endless work' (Davey 1999, p.17). This book is intended to act as an introduction or an overture (in the sense of 'opening') to this process.

An outline of the book

Chapter One surveys the various associations of 'aesthetic', the ups and downs of its philosophical history, and its changing status, from the sublime to the decadent. The influence of the association of aesthetics with decadence and perversity on both Freud and Jung's disqualification of aesthetic properties is also explained.

Chapter Two provides some philosophical background to help locate 'where' aesthetic experience might be taking place, and to suggest that its situation is essentially intermediate, in between the subjective and the objective. It also deals with the interplay between perception and imagination, the psychological lining of experience, from a phenomenological perspective, using Merleau-Ponty's thought.

Chapter Three uses the notion that aesthetic experience is embodied, rather than being abstract or detached, as a way of exploring the range of meanings that can be conveyed by painting's material (aesthetic) properties. This leads to a critique of psychoanalytic theories about art, both in the way they detach the aesthetic from the psychological aspects of painting, and of the limited range of bodily experiences they posit as the basis for the supposedly unconscious or libidinal content of painting.

Chapter Four concentrates on Anton Ehrenzweig's theories about the 'inarticulate' substructure of painting and how this constitutes a richer and more complex type of form creation than that produced under conscious control. Painting is better able than clinical material to provide evidence of a 'hidden order' that requires the revision of many psychoanalytic ideas. Nevertheless, Ehrenzweig's concept of the role of the aesthetic remains close to its traditional function as a form of embellishment.

The connection between aesthetics and beauty is more central in Chapter Five. James Hillman's ideas about the necessary connection between aesthetics, beauty and what archetypal psychology calls the 'soul' dimension of experience is explored. But in applying this to the aesthetic and psychological features of painting, the dynamic function of 'ugliness' is crucially involved in that peculiar idiom of the psyche called 'pathologising'.

Psychopathology is the background to Chapter Six, which looks at the therapeutic aspects of art, both as a process in itself, and as a profession (art therapy). Despite its dependence on art, art therapy has been curiously reluctant to explore the links between the aesthetic qualities of artworks and their psychological meanings.

In Chapter Seven we revisit the problematic relationship between psychological aesthetics and psychoanalysis, and the different ways in which each sees the aesthetic as being embodied, in both the creation and the reception of works of art. In the end, the very notion of unconscious 'depth' is open to question, as in Lyotard's critique.

How we set about articulating aesthetic responses in words, and the leakages between description and interpretation, are the focus of Chapter Eight. Here the 'subjective' strategies of poetic writing and the scattering of images about a painting have a great deal to offer, providing they stay faithful to its material qualities.

In its Conclusion, my book tries to explore some of the implications of taking psychological aesthetics seriously: philosophy, psychology, psychoanalysis, art education and art therapy, as well as the ways we write about art in any of these contexts, could all be affected.

Endnotes

1. For a fuller discussion of this relation between 'seeing in' and representation, and the possibility that there is a 'pre-epistemic' integration of the two, see Kelly 1991.

2   While this book was in press I was delighted and encouraged to read John Armstrong's introduction to just such a creative reception of painting. He says, for example, that 'Acquaintance with a medium doesn't require just that we memorise a few propositions, it requires an imaginative feel for the physical qualities of the material and their manipulation.' (Armstrong 2000, p.33).

3. Shearer West's chapter on degeneration gives a good overall account of these tendencies (West 1993).
4. Anton Ehrenzweig gives a slightly different account of the same series of paintings (Enrenzweig 1967, pp. 156–7).

Chapter One

The Rise and Fall of the Aesthetic

I am now convinced that the highest act of reason, which embraces all Ideas, is
an aesthetic act, and that truth and goodness are brothers only in beauty ...
(System Programme of German Idealism 1796[1])

'Aesthetics' covers a vast and forbidding territory. Vast, because it includes
many arcane or disputed areas in philosophy and art history; forbidding,
insofar as it often appears to be the preserve either of abstruse theoreticians or
of self-appointed arbiters of taste. The scale of its judgements ranges from
grand arguments about the nature of beauty and its relation to truth to minute
discriminations concerning the qualities of particular works of art. There often
seems to be a tiresome gap between the immediacy of our responses to a work
and the ponderous conceptual apparatus brought in to justify or explain them.
Many times I have grown impatient with the abstract, generalising discourse of
philosophical aesthetics. On the other hand, I have sometimes felt a sense of
despair in trying to account for the specific pleasure given me by a painting to
some more sceptical spectator.

Yet aesthetic effects can seem immediate and striking. One writer has gone
so far as to assert 'Aesthetic qualities ... given concretely and directly, do not
require theoretical assumptions aside from the simplest ones which amount to
the common-sense attitude of naive realism and the trust in the credibility of
our senses' (Golaszewska 1988, p.73).

My own view is that while some basic aesthetic reactions, such as attraction,
repulsion, excitement or boredom, may exist in this immediate,
un-self-conscious way, others require more attention in order to emerge. There
is also a feedback effect between such experiences and our attempts to
articulate them. We may have to struggle to put them into words; but this can
then result in our responses being deepened and enriched, even if the cost is
sometimes one of failure or betrayal. Proust wrote about his need 'to see clearly
into my being thrilled': many passages in *A la Recherche du Temps Perdu* not only
vividly and subtly convey his aesthetic response, both to nature, and to works
of art, but enter vicariously into our own aesthetic responses.

However, for most of us the inherent difficulties of this effort to grasp our own aesthetic experience can be aggravated by an uncomfortable awareness of the standards and idiom of aesthetic discourse, whether this be philosophical, critical or even literary. I have already mentioned the lofty and often mind-boggling abstractions of much theorising. There is also the eminently respectable language of art history, with its academic authority and expertise in connoisseurship. Finally, there is the common sense impression that the discourse of the world of art is in one way or another exclusive: artists' or critics' statements can appear pretentious or provocative, and an underlying suspicion or resentment can easily be aroused in the uninitiated reader. I believe that, in the face of this array of writing that is either depersonalised and unfeeling, or opinionated and self-assertive, more personal or 'subjective' responses to works of art need to be encouraged and valued.

How are we to get our bearings in this disorienting field? There are several distinct provinces of the aesthetic that can, provisionally, be outlined. One concerns philosophical ideas about the relations between beauty and truth and the intellectual or spiritual values that depend on them. Plato's discussions about our sensuous apprehension of material form in nature or in art, and the ways in which they suggest an immaterial world of ideal forms are an obvious starting point. A second, related province is that of theoretical accounts of how aesthetic judgements are arrived at and what criteria there might be for them. As we shall see, a vast and imposing philosophical literature dealing with this built up in the late eighteenth and early nineteenth century, including Fichte, Schiller, Kant and Hegel. A third area comprises what might be called the artic- ulation of taste, and is more closely linked to prevailing stylistic fashions in art. Here discriminatory or judgemental functions come to the fore in art criticism and the sharp edge of connoisseurship.

In addition to these intellectual aspects, aesthetics is also associated with a psychological perspective that gradually takes shape as this theoretical background builds itself up. This has to do with a sophisticated relish of the senses, and, in specific relation to the visual arts, with the sheer pleasure of looking. 'Perspective' is a suggestive word here, for at first sight looking seems like the most detached and spectacular of all the senses; yet it is actually something that involves the rest of the body to a far greater extent than is usually acknowledged (as we shall see in Chapter Three). Nevertheless, in the closing years of the nineteenth century, an 'aesthetic' appreciation of either nature or art concentrated on the most sophisticated forms of sensory experience, ones that were deliberately distanced from everyday experience.

The extremity, in every sense, of this position is shown up by theories in which more general historical or social perspectives are taken on aesthetics. For example, some Marxist critics have sought to show that aesthetic judgements which appear to be autonomous are in fact ideologically determined: in other words, what is presented as a free choice is actually the effect of socio-political or economic influences. Other writers have explored different modes of aesthetic experience at a collective level in various cultures and historical periods (Tuan 1995). More radically, other thinkers – significantly, from the realm of psychotherapy – have put forward the necessity of re-sensitising our aesthetic responses to the environment, whether natural or man-made, if ecological or political catastrophe is to be avoided (Hillman 1982; Moore 1996; Sardello 1992).

All of this can seem a long way removed from individual paintings and the particular kinds of responses they evoke in us. It also seems to set up an opposition between the interior or subjective aspect of aesthetics, symbolised by the aggressively irresponsible stance of 'decadent' art, and a more external or public face, symbolised by current ecologically oriented aesthetics. It is almost as if imaginative life must be either introverted or extraverted. But to situate imaginative life in a purely interior realm is already to ratify a divorce between 'inner' and 'outer' realities which the nature of aesthetic experience in fact contradicts, as will be shown in Chapter Two.

Imaginative life, and the aesthetic responses that are a part of it, depend instead upon an intermediate space in between 'inner' and 'outer' realities. Aesthetic qualities are incubated, as it were, in this space and eventually brought to light. Perhaps it was just such a space that Rilke (1914) had in mind when he wrote:

> One single space runs through all being
>
> World-inner-space. Silent, the birds fly
>
> Through and beyond us. O, what I will to grow
>
> I see outside, and in me grows the tree.

> (my translation)

If aesthetic response were really an entirely inner world experience, then it would be difficult or impossible to communicate. But while our aesthetic responses certainly have features that are inarticulate, or even 'beyond words', these should not be identified too quickly with experiences that are essentially subjective or uncommon.

There are some analogies here between the intermediate status of aesthetic experience and dreams. Dreams make use of what psychoanalysis calls 'day residues', fragments of events from the dreamer's external world. They are also marked by what could be called a personal idiom or signature that is characteristic of the individual dreamer: at the same time they can be shown to deploy symbolic vocabularies that have a more general currency (sexual, political, even artistic). But unlike dreams, in our aesthetic response to a painting we each have a common starting point: the work itself, which provides a visible yardstick against which our various accounts can be compared.

Thus aesthetic responses have an objective side to them, insofar as they are founded on the actual qualities of things in the world, whether they be works of nature or of art. In addition, the language or discourse of aesthetic experience, however far-fetched it may sometimes feel, establishes and confirms a realm that is more than subjective. Furthermore, language does not simply report aesthetic experience: it can also enhance and promote it, in the sense of taking it further (as we shall see in Chapter Eight). Like the literature of dreams, where a culture of dream experience is elaborated, writing (or indeed reading) about aesthetic experiences can nurture a capacity for creative response.

There are a number of problems here which I want to introduce straight-away even if they may be further explored elsewhere in this book. One has to do with the nature of the expressive traffic between a spectator and a painting. When we call passages of paint, or whole works, 'sad' or 'cheerful' we seem to be saying that there is something in the work that makes us, and perhaps other viewers, feel that way. It might seem that we then have to choose between two alternatives. One is that this sadness was originally in the artist's mind, at some level, and that it amounts to an expression or a communication that can be backed up by his or her intentions. The other is that the feeling is in our minds, and must therefore be a projection.

But this 'sadness' itself might not be as straightforward an emotional response as it seems. It is not just that the 'feeling' involved may not easily fit into pigeon holes of our emotional vocabulary: it could be more of a metaphor for something about the material qualities of the painting itself, and these might be independent of either our state of mind or that of the artist.[2] So the feelings we have are not always the result of projection, nor are they necessarily a communication or expression from the artist: some of these feelings are a response to qualities inherent in a painting that have an independent existence.

However, if there is either no statement from the artist who made it, or else one that points in a quite different direction, do we have any real warrant for attributing a particular expressive or aesthetic quality to a work of art? A door seems to open here that would let any and every interpretation in, no matter how arbitrary or far-fetched. The idea that a painting could have meanings that differ from the artist's expressed intentions is a major stumbling-block for popular assumptions that the artist is, or should be, solely responsible for its meaning.[3] The popular image of the artist seems to be polarised between those who have a professional technique with which they can produce the desired effects and those who abandon all control in a sort of creative lottery.

But if artists only measured the success of their work by the extent to which it matched their 'intentions', however those might be defined, and did not hope that what they made would also surprise them, art would have a pretty limited interest. And if the main purpose of art was simply to 'communicate' to others messages about states of mind or body, or about intended themes (existential, moral, political and so forth), its interest would be similarly reduced. The life of a work of art depends upon its independence, upon its being able to continue to generate new meanings long after its original creation; and this in turn depends upon its material aesthetic properties.

To put forth a work of art into the world is to have to relinquish control over what may be done with it. This is a familiar motif in creation myths (including the Biblical story of Paradise), and is perhaps one of the reasons why so-called 'outsider' artists guard their privacy so jealously. However, it is not just the public exhibition, but the actual material creation of art that makes it escape its creator's control. This is not just a matter of obvious or dramatic 'unconscious' creation (as in the cliché image of Action Painting). By the very process of creating a work that exists in the external world, any artist has made it to some extent independent of him. It is inevitably other: it may even feel foreign or unrecognisable to him.[4]

Part of this estrangement has also to do with the translation between mental states or events and painting that creating a work of art involves. A work of art can never be the same as a mental state: however powerful the experience or intention that prompts it may be, a painting is a material artifact with its own distinct properties. An obvious example is a certain type of Surrealist painting, exemplified by Salvador Dali's 'hallucinatory' pictures, which seem almost to illustrate Freud's theories about the function of images in dream and phantasy.[5] Yet even these works, which invite and play with an illusionistic response, have a glassy, submarine facture, a liquid technique, that is a crucial part of their effect.

A brief history of aesthetics

With these problems in mind, I want to return to the notion of 'aesthetic' from a more theoretical and historical perspective. Since the mid-eighteenth century, theories about aesthetics and claims about the fundamental nature of aesthetic experience or the value to be set upon it have ridden something of a rollercoaster career from the most elevated to the most effete, from the sublime to the ridiculous. What was once seen, in the earlier phases of this trajectory, as one of the highest functions of the human mind, chosen by Kant to be the essential index of human freedom, had acquired, by the end of the nineteenth century, connotations of elitism, preciosity and even perversity.

It is this latter-day image of the aesthetic that Freud and Jung refer to when, in the opening decades of the twentieth century, they propose new ways of understanding the psychological import of works of art in terms of an unconscious dimension to pictorial imagery. Both treat aesthetic appeal as a purely formal, surface phenomenon that is indeed seductive and misleading, and has little or nothing to do with a work's underlying psychological significance.

In the course of time, there have also been significant shifts in what is meant by 'aesthetic'. In a broad historical perspective, aesthetics is to begin with a branch of philosophy, concerned with giving some account of what gives works of art interest or value. In Plato's thought this is bound up with the relation between art, beauty and the world of ideal forms; but by the same token the appeal of art (particularly visual art) to the senses is inherently suspect.[6] Later accounts of the aesthetic – for example those in English writers such as Shaftesbury, Hutcheson or Hume – focus more on the actual nature of aesthetic experience[7]. This shift from the criterion of aesthetics being its objective relation to invisible, transcendent ideals, to a closer association of aesthetics with more internal or subjective aspects of experience, will prepare the way for later psychological or even scientific investigations into the nature of such experience.

The actual term 'aesthetic' dates from Baumgarten's *Aesthetica*, published in two parts in the 1750s.[8] To begin with the term appeared to concern the philosophical status of our sensuous grasp of the world, in all its particularity.[9] In 1790 a far more ambitious concept of the aesthetic appeared in Kant's *Third Critique of Judgement*, where it played a crucial role in bridging the gap between intellectual knowledge and sensuous apprehension. At the same time, Kant introduced the idea that there was something necessarily disinterested about aesthetic experience: that is, that it served no obvious use or function. Nevertheless, the universality claimed by Kant for aesthetic judgement is partly justified by its object displaying what he calls 'the form of purposiveness'. This is a peculiarly difficult and paradoxical concept, which is almost like a nobler precursor of the 'aimless logic' that Hans Prinzhorn lists as one of the characteristic features of early twentieth century psychotic art.[10]

In Kant's and other eighteenth and nineteenth century thinkers' philosophies (including Schelling and Schopenhauer) aesthetic judgment and the experience of beauty occupy a high place. For Kant it exemplified the prototypical exercise of human freedom. Several other issues are also involved, which give aesthetics an importance that extends beyond the realm of art alone. In particular, there is the question of whether art and nature are to be included within the same aesthetic perspective, or whether art in some way condenses aspects of our aesthetic appreciation of nature. The latter involves the issue of what kind of transformation or translation might be involved in this decanting or siphoning of our experience of the world into an art form, and this will be explored in Chapter Two.

Rather than going over each theorist in this newly established field of philosophical aesthetics in detail, I shall simply select some of its salient features, without any attempt to synthesise them, in order to highlight some of the main issues involved, and to suggest how many of them appear in a different light when seen from a psychological rather than a philosophical perspective. This is hardly surprising, since the category of the 'psychological', in the sense of that which has to do with introspective access to 'inner' states of imagination, reverie or phantasy, all of which are involved in aesthetic experience, is a relatively modern one.

First of all, aesthetic experience is necessarily sensuous, it engages with the particular features of an object: yet at the same time it situates this detail within a more general framework of understanding (Baumgarten). This sensuous idiom may be better conveyed by images than by language, and translated in terms of feeling rather than of concepts (Hamann). Aesthetic cognition serves no extraneous purpose: by the same token it is also an index of free human subjectivity and its autonomous mode of validating knowledge. Yet it is at the same time a bridge between the understanding and imagination and as such transcends merely logical laws (Kant). The materialisation involved in the production of the objects of aesthetic experience is a crucial mode of self-actualisation; and it can be developed from mere individual play into a shared system of values (Schelling).

Even in this summary and partial list one can pick up a contrast between aesthetic experience as an embodied and sensuous involvement with material texture and form, and a more abstract or philosophical aesthetics, one of whose ambitions is to justify art as a form of knowledge. It is evident that aesthetics deals on the one hand with specific and actual responses to individual works of art, and on the other with questions of the general principles according to which such particular experiences can be made sense of. The gap between the two needs to be bridged, not only by theory getting to grips with actual artworks, but also by our trying to articulate our aesthetic response more fully.

One of the problems raised by this connection between the particular and the general is how individual responses, which often involve intense investment of feeling, can be knitted together into a more comprehensive intellectual or theoretical account. In other words, can we locate these particular instances, with all their passionate idiosyncrasy and personal colouring, in some more objective framework that will justify them and give them an inter-subjective coherence?

Some of the earliest attempts to do this were in terms theories of 'taste' (such as Sulzer's 'Allgemeine Theorie der schönen Künste' of 1771–4[11]). Here there is a two-way relation between taste in general, the cultivation of good sense, decorum and a predilection for the harmonious and orderly, and what amount to rules for the aesthetic appreciation of both nature and art. Suitably developed taste governs our response to art and conversely, acquaintance with the right kind of art develops our taste. Sulzer even goes so far as to define aesthetics as 'the science of the feelings'. This issue, of what sort of feelings are admissible in aesthetic response, and of the extent to which they are bound up with harmonious or beautiful forms, is one that persistently crops up in aesthetic theory, and it will become peculiarly problematic both when Modernism challenges conventional notions of beauty and when psychoanalysis proposes a very different 'science of the feelings'.

The metaphysical aspect of what could be called theoretical aesthetics, as articulated in the work of philosophers such as Kant, Fichte or Schelling, depends a good deal on a tacit assumption that both the nature of aesthetic judgement and the criteria it employs have a shared and recognisable common ground. Even if this collective agreement is itself arguably the preserve of a relatively privileged class, it is supposed to obey certain laws and thus to have universal validity. The cultural and artistic standards to which it appealed still had sufficient coherence in the eighteenth and nineteenth centuries to make this claim appear plausible.

But mere consensual agreement is not sufficient to buttress the high status and exemplary function of aesthetic judgement. Kant, in his *Third Critique of Judgement*, strove to assert, on the one hand its autonomous and disinterested character and its purely formal nature, and on the other to show how it necessarily connects with conceptual and moral regularities. In the difficulties surrounding his account we can already see how easily its sensuous and pleasurable aspects can separate out from its intellectual or moral functions, and how precarious the balance is between the freedom that is necessary for aesthetic judgement and some kind of responsibility in which it needs somehow to be grounded.[12]

The notion of aesthetic experience as having a given, common basis that would be the grounds for a general measure of agreement (as in Kant), or that might serve as an instrument for improving man (as in Schiller's (1954) *On the Aesthetic Education of Man*) is a 'democratic' one. It is associated with a Romantic and Idealist perspective from which it seemed as if oppositions between individual and cosmos, science and art could be superseded (for example, in the work of Goethe or Novalis). It is interesting that this is also the historical root of many ideas about the healing or therapeutic features of art.[13] But barely a century later the aesthetic had come to mean something far less generous or optimistic. This contrary (in every sense) version was an ultra-sophisticated, deliberately anti-social style of aesthetic experience that magnified the distance between the 'aesthetic attitude' and ordinary life.

This aggressively subjective mode of aesthetics was partly a result of the increasing, and to some extent deliberate, alienation of early Modernist or avant-garde art from ordinary bourgeois experience. It has an ambiguous, double aspect. On the one hand it seeks out the most refined, exquisite forms, wanting them to be unsullied by any taint of common life or vulgar appetite; on the other, it cultivates a taste for the peculiar, unusual or exotic, to the point where the quest for the exceptional and the bizarre tips into perversity. The norms and conventions it reacts against are not just formal ones: the notion that aesthetic experience is in some way a vehicle for moral or ethical values is also rejected. It is as if the exalted claims that were made only a century before have been replaced with naked snobbery and elitism, and hedonistic and self-indulgent pursuits substituted for the improving effects of the cultivation of 'good taste'.

Aesthetics in early psychoanalysis

This decadent and provocative, fin-de-siècle image of aestheticism, incarnated in figures such as Oscar Wilde or Huysman's *Des Esseintes*, is, I believe, responsible for the suspicion or outright condemnation of a work's aesthetic appeal to be found, in different forms, in both Freud and Jung. One of the many effects of the new psychoanalytic thinking is to replace the metaphysical ideals associated with earlier theories of aesthetics with psychological motivations that have their roots in powerful unconscious fantasies of bodily gratification. Aesthetic qualities that once had an other-worldly aura are now brought brutally down to earth: their disinterested character is shown to be merely a cover for frankly instinctual impulses and unconscious infantile wishes.

In Freud's early writings on art, aesthetic pleasure is simply a superficial lure or 'cashback offer', with which the artist disguises the otherwise objectionable or narcissistic content of his work:

> The writer softens the egotistical character of the day-dream by changes and disguises, and he bribes us by the offer of a purely formal, that is, aesthetic, pleasure in the presentation of his phantasies. The increment of pleasure which

is offered us in order to release yet greater pleasure arising from deeper sources in the mind is called an 'incitement premium' or technically 'fore-pleasure' (Freud 1908).

Here the aesthetic appeal of a work of art is seen as an attractive and distracting wrapping for its more unpalatable unconscious symbolic content.

In many ways Freud's concept of unconscious symbolism is not of a deep symbolism in the sense of something that cannot be translated without serious loss: on the contrary, it is derived from a comparatively narrow range of libidinal or infantile scenarios that can be made explicit, however laborious the translation. These symbols amount to a common stock of figures: analogies, visual and verbal puns, metonymies and so on. The hidden content of these figures – their sexual or aggressive implications – is effectively identical, whatever the stylistic dress they are presented in. So in a work of art, their aesthetic cladding is irrelevant to its (unconscious) psychological meaning; indeed, aesthetic 'forepleasure', like the preliminaries in a joke, serves mainly to distract from the work's hidden meaning.

At this point aesthetic pleasure has come to be identified with response to a work's formal qualities, and for Freud these in themselves carry no psychological weight. Elsewhere he suggests that, particularly in the case of painting, they are a primitive form of gratification, only redeemed by the kind of skillful and cultural processing that is equivalent to 'work'. This relegation of aesthetic appeal to a marginal function also reflects Freud's figurative bias. His theories of unconscious symbolism, in both dream and art, revolve around a repertoire of analogical or symbolic 'figures', most of which are substitutes for sexual parts or sexual actions, which forms a sort of unconscious iconography in which what is (mis)represented is of more significance than how it is represented. To put it another way: content is all-important and form is only peripherally involved, for example in such devices as visual punning or analogy.[14]

What is more, the 'conditions of representability' that govern the translation of unconscious 'thoughts' into image form (the famous 'pictorialisation of thoughts' in dreams) are actually themselves derived from the conventions of representational art, as are the figurative devices of the dream-work (condensation, displacement, substitution and so forth). It is this figurative vocabulary of unconscious thought and the economy of its compression and over-determination that are the main objects of Freud's attention: their stylistic or aesthetic features are treated as marginal or irrelevant.

It is no accident that Freud's conservative view of art's psychological significance and his privileging of its unconscious iconography over its formal or material qualities appear at the very same time as the first attempts to develop a new theory of aesthetics based on precisely those 'surface' features that he disqualifies. It is these intrinsic formal qualities of works of art that are the focus of Clive Bell's contemporary notion of 'significant form', for example, which first appeared in his book *Art* of 1914.

Bell's claim that aesthetic experience is a response to the intrinsic formal structure of visual works of art locates the psychologically expressive factors of a painting in its actual 'painterly' qualities, and is thus a kind of mirror-image of the Freudian reading in which psychological depth is set off against aesthetic surface. At the same time, Bell's concept of significant form, because it is no longer dependent on representational or symbolic readings, can concentrate on the compositional elements of a work of art. It moves us from the belief that a work of art evokes or symbolises something beyond itself, which it can only partially embody, or to which it can only refer through some kind of figurative ventriloquism, to the idea that an essential part of its significance is materially embodied in its form, structure and 'handwriting'. We shall see later that this shift is crucial to the development of a new psychological aesthetics.

Meanwhile, another, and different, misunderstanding of aesthetic qualities is to be found in Jung. This is something of a surprise, since one of his major differences from Freud consists in the fact that he considered that image was primary in a number of ways: it was the most immediate form in which the psyche presented itself (in the phantasy idiom of what he called 'non-directed thinking'), and it was also, in the form of archetypal symbols, the most complex and inexhaustible source of psychological insight.

On the basis of his own experience, Jung believed that unconscious material, surfacing in the form of a mood, could be given shape through the technique of 'creative formulation': in other words through the materialisation of an image. This is spelt out in his *The Transcendent Function* (Jung 1960), originally written in 1916. Indeed in one passage it looks as if Jung sees the working out of formal and psychological factors as going hand in hand: 'Image and meaning are identical; and as the former takes shape, so the latter becomes clear. Actually the pattern needs no interpretation: it betrays its own meaning' (p. 204).

This seems to make an inextricable link between formal (aesthetic) and symbolic (psychological) features. It also implies that the working out need not be an immediate or spontaneous process for unconscious or archetypal meanings to surface.

But despite pioneering the use of image-making in a therapeutic context, Jung felt compelled to point out the dangers of treating such productions as art and to warn against the insidious effect of what he called 'the aesthetic attitude'. To consider oneself an artist simply because one has created remarkable images from out of the unconscious is to risk being narcissistically entranced by their superficial appeal and thus blinded to the psychological or ethical demands implicit in them. 'The danger of the aesthetic tendency is over-valuation of the formal or 'artistic' worth of the phantasy-productions; the libido is diverted from the real goal of the transcendent function and side-tracked into purely aesthetic problems of artistic expression' (Jung 1960, p.84).

In Chapter Eight of *Memories, Dreams and Reflections* (1963), Jung gives a dramatic reconstructed account of his own struggle against this temptation, and portrays himself as fighting to maintain the distinction between art (typically represented by a seductive anima figure) with its involvement with the aesthetic, and science, the rock Jung himself clung to, with its concern for the psychological.

In his work with the paintings his patients brought him, Jung seems to have been more interested in the figurative and archetypal resonances of the pictures, or in formal features such as their geometrical symbolism (the combi-nation of circular and quadrangular motifs is a crucial feature of mandala imagery) than in their specific aesthetic qualities. Yet the actual images in his few published case studies contain many passages where there are noticeable inflections of colour and form that are not accounted for by the symbolic or iconographical terms in which Jung is reading them.[15]

Early psychiatric perspectives on aesthetics

It is worth mentioning a third contemporary area in which stylistic or aesthetic properties were overlooked or misunderstood: that of the psychiatric perspec-tive on so-called 'psychotic art'. Early interpretations of artworks created by patients in insane asylums tended to align the formal features of the work – dis-tortions, repetitions, the 'cramming' of space with forms or marks (including writing) and so forth – with other symptoms of mental illness. In its most basic form this picture portrayed the psychotic artist in the grip of instinctual forces of which he or she was largely unaware. While some writers, most notably Walther Morgenthaler in his monograph on Adolf Wölfli (1992; first published in 1921), emphasised the artistic quality of psychotic art, this creativity is seen as the result of fundamental instinctual forces over which the artist has little or no control: 'His method of work conveys the impression of an urgency, an internal necessity; Wölfli seems to follow a law, to obey the ineluc-table' and later 'If one cannot speak strictly of inspiration in respect to Wölfli's art, there is still less a question of a true elaboration in his works. They emerge, so to speak, full-grown from his spirit; he throws them onto the paper without changing anything' (Morgenthaler 1992, pp.22–3).

A much more radical approach along these lines is contained in Hans Prinzhorn's daring *Artistry of the Mentally Ill*, first published a year later in 1922. Prinzhorn embarks on a complex and exhaustive analysis of the stylistic features of 'schizophrenic art' and the various ways in which they deform or exaggerate the normal artistic conventions of representation, decoration and symbolisation. In his writing there are occasional glimpses of connections between aesthetic and psychological features. For example: 'even the simplest scribble ... is, *as a manifestation of expressive gestures*, the bearer of psychic components, and the whole of psychic life lies as if in perspective behind the most insignificant form element' (Prinzhorn 1972, p.42 (my emphasis)).

No doubt this owes something to Ludwig Klages' theories of organic expressiveness as demonstrated by handwriting and other subliminal forms of signification, but it also implies a broader conception of the psychological than that espoused by either psychiatry or psychoanalysis.

Prinzhorn also made the connection between the attempt to deal with a world of 'pure psychic qualities' that was engaged with under compulsion in schizophrenia, but that also formed a crucial part of the programme of many avant-garde artists of his day. He was, however, sceptical of the capacity of an art based on '[a] liberation from the compulsion of external appearances ... so complete that all configuration should deal only with pure psychic qualities' (1972, p.272) to establish a genuine form of communication with others.

We have thus reached a point, in the first decades of the twentieth century, where there is a kind of convergence between various models of unconscious or instinctual mental functioning, their manifestation in pictorial form in a variety of seemingly separate contexts, and different notions of the nature and status of formal or aesthetic qualities. On the one hand, there is the idea that aesthetic qualities result from the deliberate application of the artist's technical skills; on the other is the idea that some of the most significant psychological qualities are connected to pictorial form in a spontaneous, automatic or unconscious way. At the same time, the notion of what 'psychological' messages a work of art is capable of conveying has also become split, between intentional or con-sciously expressed content, of a more or less conventional kind, and instinctual, automatic or 'unconscious' forms of significance, whose status is more contro-versial.

Some Modernist initiatives, that also belong to the same period, sought to collapse these distinctions. Hans Arp (1951), for example, a leading member of Zurich Dada, asserted that spontaneous, unpremeditated creation was simply 'productive' rather than reproductive, and entailed no attempt on the artist's part to communicate. Here aesthetic qualities are treated as 'pure' and unmoti-vated, having no deeper psychological resonance than that of play or experiment. A kind of mirror-image of these avant-garde provocations can be found in the conservative reactions of contemporary psychiatry, where Modernist artists as diverse as Cézanne, Kandinsky or the Expressionists were diagnosed as exhibiting schizophrenic traits on the basis of their distortion of representational conventions or their refusal to reproduce recognisable features of the external world.

The psychiatric translation of formal or aesthetic features into clinical indications of closely corresponding psychological states, that is, those of mental disturbance, depends on a set of tacit assumptions about normal or proper representation, composition and symbolisation. Yet these conventional assumptions are precisely what were undermined by Modernism. A similar set of assumptions lies behind attempts by experimental psychologists to establish a scientific basis for aesthetic response. Indeed both kinds of investigation rely on preconceptions about disturbances of 'normal' perception, and these in turn often depend upon developmental schemas (for example the progressive sophistication of children's aesthetic choices).

From this 'scientific' perspective, aesthetic reactions can be quantified by statistical measurement of the preference for particular formal combinations, such as the well-known 'golden section'. Their psychological significance is thus reduced to being average choices that are supposed to reflect fundamental laws of perception. Inevitably the questionnaire method usually adopted narrows the range of psychological response to generalised categories such as 'expression of feeling', 'harmony of colours' or 'atmospheric effect' (see for example Pickford 1972, pp.133–46).

The limitations of such experiments are similar to those involving the standardised measurement of outcomes in psychotherapy: a great deal of important qualitative information is lost in the process of rendering subjective experience amenable to statistical analysis. An analysis that averages responses out in terms of broad common denominators lacks the particularity and depth that more 'personal' accounts can provide. Indeed I shall argue that frankly 'subjective' elaborations of individual response may, when put together with other similar accounts, give us information that is both more faithful to the particular and specific aesthetic features of a work of art and phenomenologically truer to the range and depth of our psychological response to them.

Endnotes

1. This document is translated by Andrew Bowie. It was written in Hegel's hand, but seems to owe much to Schelling (Bowie 1990, pp.45–53)
2. This problem is discussed at length by Wollheim (1991, pp.51–65).

3. In the context of art therapy, this cultural stereotype reinforces the psychological resistance many patients have to relaxing the grip of intentionality on their work, both in its making and in its interpretation.

4. It may be that this phenomenon is played out in a peculiarly intense form in 'psychotic art'.

5. In a sense, Dali's work represents a logical conclusion to Freud's appropriation from traditional figurative art of 'the conditions of representability' in dreams (see Chapter Three).

6. The idea that the formal aspects of a work may exercise a seductive (aesthetic) appeal that eclipses their proper content is one that recurs both in the use of art for religious purposes and, later in the Jungian use of art for therapeutic ends.

7. George Dickie's *Introduction to Aesthetics* provides one of the best and most succinct accounts of these fundamental shifts in aesthetic theory in relation to visual art (Dickie 1997).

8. In much of what follows I am indebted to Andrew Bowie's (1990) excellent survey *Aesthetics and Subjectivity: From Kant to Nietzsche.*

9. Baumgarten's concern anticipates James Hillman's return to the ancient Greek association of aesthesis with our immmediate apprehension of the qualitative features of phenomena (see Chapter Six).

10. See Prinzhorn 1972, p.235.

11. See Anne-Marie Link 1992.

12. A useful discussion of these problems can be found in Bernstein 1992, pp.17–38.

13. See, for example, Edwards 1989.

14. The most notorious example is the 'vulture' that Oscar Pfister discovered in the folds of drapery in Leonardo's 'Virgin and St. Anne with the Infant Jesus' (The Louvre).

15. The most extensive is the case study of an American-Scandinavian woman where some 24 of her 'mandala' images are reproduced (Jung 1959).

Chapter Two

The Split between Inner and Outer Worlds and the Impoverishment of Psychological Life

A star

is as far

as the eye

can see

and

as near

as my eye

is to me

(Gregory Corso 1989, p.182)

At the end of the last chapter I spoke of the limitations of a scientific psychology of aesthetics. One problem with this scientific perspective is that its empirical approach privileges those features of aesthetic response that can be most readily quantified, and other more qualitative aspects are distorted by being treated 'objectively' or else effectively disqualified. Another, more fundamental, difficulty is that it assumes that pictorial features – proportions, lines, colours and so on – are simply 'out there' in the work of art, waiting to induce their effects, which can then be measured. Individual psychological responses can then conveniently be treated as variables in relation to these objective formal properties. While these approaches can produce interesting findings about the psycho-physiological aspects of response to a work of art, the common ground of aesthetic experience that they establish feels thin, dry and far removed from what most of us would recognise. It deals only with the outward half of such experiences, leaving their 'inner' aspects stranded in an inaccessible realm of subjectivity.

Of course our aesthetic reactions are based on particular works with actual properties that do have a material basis. As Paul Crowther (1993) reminds us:

> Although the constitution of a purely aesthetic object is a function of the cognitive activity of those who observe an artwork, we are not entitled to say it is just a function of that activity. We are guided, surely, in forming our attitude by the perceptible formal features of the work, and are able in principle to justify and argue the validity of our response by reference to them. This capacity, indeed, gives a rational community to aesthetic consciousness (p. 37).

But it is equally important not to assign these formal features a purely material or 'objective' basis, if by that is meant that their qualitative aspect somehow exists independent of us. As James Elkins (1996) writes:

> Seeing is like hunting and like dreaming, and even like falling in love. It is entangled in the passions – jealousy, violence, possessiveness; and it is soaked in affect – in pleasure and displeasure, and in pain. Ultimately, seeing alters the thing that is seen and transforms the seer. Seeing is metamorphosis, not mechanism (pp. 11–12).

Phenomenology and aesthetic experience

If seeing inevitably has a psychological lining to it, this is magnified in the case of objects to which we give a special degree of attention. A bottle of vintage Burgundy, for example, does not reveal its individual nuances of colour, nose and taste until we open it, pour out a glass and see, smell or taste it. There may be a consensus among a group of wine tasters that this particular vintage ought to have a remarkable character, and that this character should be exemplified in specific features of the wine; but no matter how impressive the background knowledge of the tasters, or how precise their vocabularies of appreciation, the wine's qualities are in a sense 'performed' at the moment of tasting. I have chosen this example because it has important features in common with the appreciation of works of art: the gradual enhancement of the perception of an object, in which both objective and subjective elements play their part, and the development of a metaphoric vocabulary that both initiates and communicates this enhancement. The notion of the 'performance' of psychoaesthetic response is one I shall return to in Chapter Eight.

A phenomenological view of the world, and in particular that exemplified in the later philosophy of Merleau-Ponty, seems to offer the most developed account of these complex transactions that cut across conventional divisions between the subjective and objective facets of lived experience. Since sight is so crucially involved with access to works of art, it is worth quoting him on the 'interweaving' (entrelac) between seer and seen: '... we know that, since sight is a feeling out through looking, it too must imprint itself on the order of being that it reveals to us; he who looks must be no stranger to the world he looks at' (Merleau-Ponty 1964, p.177, my translation).

Our experience of the visible world is therefore not just a matter of registering impressions or responding to external stimuli; it also involves the mobilisation of a whole range of psychological effects – feelings, memories, imaginative constructions of one kind or another – many of which may not enter into our conscious awareness of perception. Nor, despite the enormous emphasis in aesthetic theory on the visible surface, is this experience an exclusively visual or retinal one: as Merleau-Ponty says, the visible touches us in a number of ways. Sight and touch are thus implicated by one another:

> We must get used to the idea that any visible thing is carved out of the tangible, any tangible thing somehow destined for visibility, and that there is an overlapping, a bestriding, not only between the toucher and what is touched but also between the tangible and the visible that is encrusted therein, just as, conversely, the former is not a visual blank, is not without visual existence (Merleau-Ponty 1964, p.177, my translation)

These complexities of vision are both enhanced and transmuted when it comes to our response to works of art, to such an extent that it may be inappropriate to apply the language of ordinary sense-experience to them. I shall say more about this in Chapter Eight.

Merleau-Ponty claims that our perception of an object involves as much internal as external response, and that a painting both inscribes and recovers this:

> Quality, light, colour, depth, that are out there in front of us, are there only because they awaken an echo in our body, because it makes them welcome. This internal equivalent, this carnal recipe [formule charnelle] for their presence, that is evoked in me by things, why should they not in their turn engender a trace [tracé], one still visible, in which any other gaze could recover the themes that underly its inspection of the world? (Merleau-Ponty 1964, p.22, my translation)

In other words, there is a kind of resonance between our individual internalisations of the world and the kind of cumulative structure of marks to be found in the paintings of, for example, Cézanne.[1] I shall return later to compare Merleau-Ponty's 'carnal recipe' with other accounts of the ways in which a painting's facture can be translated into imaginative identifications of various types.

Looking at a painting is, therefore, something even more complicated than looking at a more ordinary object:

> I would have some real difficulty in saying where the painting I am looking at is, for I do not look at it as one looks at some thing, I do not pin it in its place, my gaze wanders about in it as if in the auras of Being, rather than seeing it, I see via it or with it (Merleau-Ponty 1964, p.23, my translation).

This participation in seeing has crucial implications for our understanding of aesthetic response. To some extent it is something of which we are largely unconscious: we 'read' a picture, we have learned to see into or through it so fluently that it often takes a considerable effort to replay the process consciously, as it were in slow motion.

'Wandering about' painting

Even when a painting seems to strike us immediately, and to present itself all at once, more comprehensively than, for example, a text, it can still be shown experimentally that this impression is dependent on a complex set of saccadic eye movements. More often, our apprehension of a painting oscillates between global and local takes. Hence we can exercise a certain amount of choice over how far we allow ourselves to 'wander about' in a painting. In this respect painting is perhaps an art more vulnerable to carelessness or indifference than, for example, music. Music can enter into us more immediately, whereas the intimate transactions of our response to painting need more time to work, or rather, a time that is not so simply imposed on us from outside.

This 'wandering about' in a painting has to do with what I shall call our imaginative inhabitation of it, and it is this that gives it a depth or resonance of meaning: in other words, our response to its material aesthetic properties has a continuous psychological lining to it. These subliminal reverberations are far more various than what is usually comprehended under the psychoanalytic label of 'unconscious'. They actually take place on a number of levels simultaneously, and some of these are quite difficult to unpack. These levels can be roughly sorted out into a general, overall compositional level, a more local level of form, and finally a level of the particular close-up detail (down to a few square inches). Of course all these levels overlap and interact, but in describing our response to painting we tend to focus on any one of them in turn.

Jackson Pollock's work provides some good examples of this occurring at each level. A large 'drip' painting, such as One: Number 31, 1950 will display this on the overall compositional scale; a smaller 'cut-out' painting will exhibit it on the more local scale (within the cut-out form); and an earlier painting like Eyes in the Heat (1946) will show it at the micro-level of its almost indecipherable facture. At whatever level, the more indeterminate the form, the more 'unconscious' the mode of response, and the more powerful its psychological effects are likely to be (as we shall see in Chapter Four).

Within each of these levels, there is no doubt a deeply unconscious mode of response, where distinctions between subject and other bodily sensations and thinking or feeling may not yet be articulated. This mode could be called 'pre-epistemic' (Kelly 1991) or it might be said to belong to a 'maternal' realm that is 'pre-symbolic' in the sense that the separation between subject and object upon which conventional symbolism depends has not evolved or is in suspense (Kristeva 1980). It is most obviously evoked by paintings whose 'informality' seems both to call forth and to echo these unbounded experiences.

Obviously, in many other, less dramatic examples of painting there can be a conventional mode of organisation at one level (for example, the compositional) and a less differentiated mode at another (such as that of local facture). For example, in some of Monet's haystack paintings of the 1890s, there are local passages of colour that are not unlike the colour and brushwork of an abstract Philip Guston painting from the 1950s, but they are contained within a standard composition, a theme upon which Monet played aesthetic variations.[2] For many people such a conventional format 'contains' the potentially unsettling psychological effect of these more 'painterly' passages, which is both exciting and disturbing.

'Wandering about' in a painting in these and other ways is both a learned and a shared experience: it is a strange mixture of the solitary and the collective, the subjective and the 'trans-subjective'. As a writer who is both a painter and a Lacanian analyst recently put it:

> In aesthetic-artistic and transferential co-poiesis, a metramorphic [her own term] trans-scription of encounter occurs. Such a cross-inscription concerns artists and viewers facing the artwork in different times and places, in action and re-action. Engravings of affected events of others and of the world are unknowingly inscribed in me and mine are inscribed in others, known or anonymous, in an asymmetrical exchange that creates and transforms a trans-subjective matrixial alliance (Lichtenberg Ettinger 1999, p.25).

This 'matrixial' order is reminiscent of Kristeva's 'maternal' realm, in that it is anterior to the separations and gaps associated with the Symbolic order, in its Lacanian sense. The fact that aesthetic experience is 'trans-subjective' gives it, as we shall see, an important common ground with psychoanalytic experience, in which various kinds of 'communication' occur between what are usually thought of as being mutually inaccessible subjectivities.

But whether another person is involved, explicitly or implicitly (for example in the way in which even our internal use of language involves others), there is still a sense in which any 'seeing' involves a kind of dialogue with what is being looked at. This can be thought of as opening ourselves to its presence, to the face it presents, even to the extent of being addressed by it. Merleau-Ponty (1964) writes:

> So that the see-er is caught up in what he sees, it is still himself that he sees: there is a fundamental narcissism to all vision; and so, for the same reason, he experiences the vision he exercises as coming from the side of things, so, as many painters have observed, I feel myself looked at by things ... not to see in the external, as others see it, the contour of a body one inhabits, but above all to be seen by it, to dwell in it, to emigrate to it, to be seduced, caught, distracted by the phantom, to the extent that see-er and seen mutualise each other [se reciproquent] and that one no longer knows who is seeing and who is seen (p.183, my translation).

Certainly this experience is sometimes concentrated, intensified and prolonged in looking at painting, and one of its mysteries is that we cannot tell whether the intensity of its gaze or address comes from an other (the artist) or from the other (this peculiar object in the world).

Many of these effects, in relation to painting, are, as we have seen, subliminal, in the sense that we are more aware of their effects than of the process that gave rise to them. These include not only the fluctuating establishment of forms (fluctuating because, as we shall see, unless they are clearly outlined in Gestalt terms they are constantly open to renegotiation) and the various accompanying levels of anxiety or entrancement; but also the induction of mood, the diffusion of feeling (in more than just its emotional sense) and other aspects of the work that may be arrived at intuitively rather than rationally.

We also recreate a painting's history, in terms of imagining what might have given rise to its marks, brushstrokes and other features of its handling. This reconstruction may also be only partly conscious, depending, for example, on how much we know of the practice of painting. It may not necessarily correspond to what actually took place, but it is not on that account alone invalid (a point I shall return to in Chapter Eight). Again, the fact that such 'histories' are not to be taken in a purely technical sense makes their psychological dimension more accessible.[3]

Finally, there are responses that may be largely to do with the painting's visible significance: these do not just revolve around its explicit representational or symbolic content, they also include less conscious 'figurative' readings or associations. Such constructions may give rise to narratives or asso-ciations, conjured up either in the form of phantasies or of memories. These feel natural and immediate because they tap into a reservoir of figurative imagery which fits the way in which we are used to constructing an 'inner world' (Maclagan 1989a), but some of them may have a largely anecdotal or associa-tive connection with a painting's actual material qualities, as opposed to its subject matter.

Because abstract works do not offer the same sort of foothold for this figurative colonisation, they might be thought to offer the chance for 'purer' forms of psychoaesthetic response. Perhaps this is also the reason why many people find it harder to respond to them; but this may also be because they have resonances at a deeper, embodied or unconscious level.[4] Nevertheless, it seems that having dispensed with the alibis of representation, the artist is free to follow exactly that 'concern with line, colour and form for their own sake' of which Freud so vigorously disapproved. Kandinsky, for example, claimed that 'The contents [of painting] are indeed what the spectator lives or feels while under the effect of the forms or colour combinations of the picture.' (quoted Lindsay and Vergo 1982, p.402). Kandinsky's theories about art, and about the intrinsic properties of forms and colours, can easily be mistaken for recipes for how to produce certain spiritual effects in the spectator: but they can better be understood as his own way of accounting for their psychoaesthetic effects.

Psychoanalysis and the in-between nature of aesthetic experience

Psychoanalytic practice, which, as we have seen, hinges on intersubjective and trans-subjective aspects of experience, has much in common with the inter-weaving that I have been suggesting is so crucial to aesthetic experience. In fact this common ground is much greater than in the various attempts made in 'applied psychoanalysis' to treat works of art as windows through which glimpses of the artist's unconscious world can be stolen. Indeed, psychoanal-ysis, in giving a justifiable account of its clinical work, can be said to labour under many of the same difficulties as aesthetics:

A discourse about the unrepresentable, a praxis of the unrepresentable, aesthetics and psychoanalysis have more than one point in common. Cease-lessly confronted with the mystery of the flesh and incarnation, aesthetics has the impossible task of explaining the ineffable. Aimed at representing human suffering, which by its nature exceeds all attempts at representation, psycho-analysis, for its part, seems to chase after some difficult incarnation (Gagnebin 1994, p.31, my translation).

In other words, both aesthetics and psychoanalysis have to deal with effects that are subliminal or unconscious, that depend upon various kinds of leakage between subjective and objective realities, and that are often almost beyond the reach of language.

Early psychoanalytic accounts of the nature of our response to works of art leaned heavily on models in which the boundary between inner and outer reality is criss-crossed by processes of projection and identification. In this context, the artist performs an essentially vicarious function for the spectator (Freud 1908). Put simply, spectators respond consciously to the artist's intentions and to the aesthetic qualities with which he has enveloped them; but they also respond at an unconscious level, and therefore more powerfully, to the phantasies that underly this attractive surface, as well as identifying with the artist's 'mastery' in being able to manipulate such material. The work of art is thus to some extent an unconscious communication between two people's inner worlds.

A similar kind of communication takes place in the actual clinical setting of psychoanalysis. In transference and counter-transference the patient's unconscious and the therapist's unconscious are in subliminal contact with one another. As Christopher Bollas (1993) puts it, 'To be touched by the other's unconscious is to be scattered by the winds of the primary process to faraway associations and elaborations, reached through the private links of one's own subjectivity' (p.45).

The word 'communication' has here to be understood not as a deliberately sent message, but as a kind of resonance or echo between two adjacent chambers, or as an opening between the two (somewhat as rooms are said to 'communicate' via a door). Could there be an analogy along these lines, with the kinds of communication between a spectator and the artist via a work of art?

Obviously, the analytic situation is one between two people who are present to each other in an on-going relationship, whereas the artist's presence has to be deduced from their work, however long our acquaintance with it may be. But in both cases there is the issue of whether what we impute to the other is not simply a matter of projection. In both situations there are circumstantial factors that contain and anchor projections: on the one hand the analysand's history and the repertoire of unconscious influences, and on the other the artist's history and the repertoire of artistic conventions. However, even within these frameworks there is always the possibility of making unwarranted constructions.

The problem is aggravated once we consider that a painting might not be invested with any explicit meaning by the artist, or that its meaning might be different from that intended. But allowing a painting to be seen by others is, like psychoanalysis is for the patient, a way of opening it to a range of meaning that is unpredictable by the artist. What limits are there to this? Are all possible readings possible (as one French critic once told me), or must we have some form of conventional scaffolding within which marks can be read as expressive (as Gombrich (1963b) has argued)? Is the only alternative to be left like Polonius, guessing at the figures in clouds?

But the truth is more often a mixture of subjective and objective components, and the latter are precisely the constraints provided by the cloud's, or the work of art's, particular form. It is as if they give a shape to our feelings. As Adrian Stokes (1973) once put it:

> There are a thousand and one gradations between the power, as we feel it, of the object to suggest associations to us and the imputation, as we feel it, of our mood to this object. Anyone who, looking at clouds, with or without conscious phantasy, is increasingly arrested by the shape, tone, disposition, or the spaces between them, by every detail and its interrelation, experiences an aesthetic sensation. In asserting this, I am presuming that conscious phantasy [projection], if it makes an appearance, does not merely use the condition of the clouds as a point of departure but that, on the contrary, the movements of phantasy or of judgement have been transposed into, and therefore restricted by, the very particular visual and tactile terms of these cloudy forms: only an animating content that exalts of sharpens the shape and detail of the clouds is felicitous or aesthetic (p.114).

This notion of transposition, or as I shall call it 'translation' is crucial to our understanding of the complicated transactions between 'inner' events (thoughts, feelings, sensations) and the 'outer' ones involved in painting (see Chapter Seven). We shall also see how crucial this attention to specifics is in relation to dealing with the image in the imaginal psychology of James Hillman (see Chapter Five).

In this context it is significant that psychoanalysis is now beginning to acknowledge the subjective and intersubjective nature of its data. For example, in a recent paper it was suggested that '... the science which is still being argued about by analysts bears little resemblance to science in its contemporary definition, particularly in terms of how both subjectivity and intersubjectivity are permissibly – in fact necessarily – aspects of what makes for scientific knowledge' (Mayer 1996, p.712).

Such scientific knowledge of what is going on in psychoanalysis depends, not upon the adoption of 'objective' techniques inappropriate to the kind of intersubjective facts involved, but upon the integrity and conscientiousness of the observer.

This is similar to the way in which aesthetic experience and its psychological accompaniments have a subjective 'inside' that can nevertheless be reported or shared with skill and accuracy. Here at least the situation is simpler, in the sense that it is an object (the work of art) that is being responded to, rather than the inferred inner world of another person. However, the work of art has a peculiar status, in that it is usually expected to bear the expressive imprint of another person and is therefore often responded to as something almost half-way between a person and an object. In any case, in both instances giving an authentic account of such encounters involves a fidelity to phenomena that is at one and the same time scrupulous and imaginative: 'We need rigorously to promote ... environments which maximally facilitate frank and open reporting of all that we really think and really do in our consulting rooms, especially open reporting of all that may feel most worrisome to reveal, precisely because of how intimately subjective and intersubjective they are' (Mayer 1996, p.716).

I shall have more to say later about equivalents for this 'reporting' in terms of tuning in to the specific aesthetic qualities of an artwork; but they constitute a kind of creative reception similar to, but somewhat different from, psychoanalytic accounts of intersubjective relationships.

However, this idea of the status of aesthetic experience being neither purely objective nor utterly subjective does have one outstandingly important precursor in psychoanalytic theory. In his *Playing and Reality*, Donald Winnicott (1974) famously described the area of interaction between mother and infant as a 'transitional' or 'intermediate' space. It is an area in which the child's earliest creative gestures are recognised and responded to by the mother, and a realm of 'illusion' sustained, where no distinction is drawn between what is created from inner need and what is found in external reality. The sustained experience thus provides the capacity for play, in other words for the conjunction of inner impulse with objects in the outer world, and for experiences which therefore have a meaningful quality. This was, he claimed, also the prerequisite for later cultural experience.

> My claim is that if there is a need for this double statement [of objective and subjective realities], there is also need for a triple one: the third part of the life of a human being, a part that we cannot ignore, is an intermediate area of experiencing, to which inner reality and external life both contribute. It is an area that is not challenged, because no claim is made on its behalf except that it shall exist as a resting-place for the individual engaged in the perpetual human

task of keeping inner and outer reality separate yet interrelated (Winnicott 1974, p.3).

So the indeterminate, 'in-between' status of this 'third area' is crucial to the later capacity to enjoy the suspension of everyday reality-testing in moments of special communion, whether religious or artistic. Winnicott's concepts here are closer to a phenomenological description than to a consistently worked-out position (he was after all a paediatrician not a philosopher), but they have been of great encouragement to those who feel cramped in the dualistic framework of projective psychology or its psychotherapeutic extensions. Writers like Marion Milner, herself an artist, a psychologist and a psychoanalyst, have further explored this quality of experience in adult aesthetic response. Milner talks about the creative collaboration between conscious and unconscious processes, and the capacity to surrender, or allow the self to be temporarily dissolved, that is an essential condition for this (Milner 1987, pp.207–215).

As Milner has pointed out, the erasure of boundaries between inside and out, that is a part both of the experience of creating art and of our creative response to it, has something in common with mystical or ecstatic states. Such experiences can also incorporate a kind of positive 'madness', in the sense of an experience of fusion with the artwork. As Michael Eigen (1991) says

> To the overly operational or objective attitude, transitional experience must seem a bit mad. Similarly, the subjectively enclosed individual might idealise transitional experiencing but actually find it threatening and disorganising. Both must let go of one-sided madness to tolerate the sort of paradoxical madness Winnicott treasured, the madness associated with creative living and the birth of culture (p.80).

I do not think it far-fetched or exaggerated to suggest that some aspects of aesthetic response involve an experience of rapture or 'madness' in which there is sometimes a magical coincidence between hitherto unknown parts of oneself and the specific material qualities of another's work of art.

But there are, in the psychoanalytic tradition, other ways of talking about the two-way traffic between artwork and spectator that do not entail such dramatic revisions. Christopher Bollas (1987) has written about the capacity of objects to be 'transformational' for a person:

> The aesthetic moment constitutes this deep rapport between subject and object and provides the person with a generative illusion of fitting with an object, evoking an existential memory. Existential, as opposed to cognitive, memory is conveyed not through visual or abstract thinking, but through the affects of being. Such moments feel familiar, uncanny, sacred, reverential, and outside cognitive coherence (p.40).

This idea of the profound connections between aesthetic response and pre-representational levels of experience is something about which I shall have more to say in the next chapter.

It is interesting that Bollas (1993) also writes about the characteristic ways in which individuals select objects to induce certain psychic effects, and of how this constitutes an 'idiom': '... the choice of form is a kind of psychic route, as each subject, possessing many different forms for the collecting of experience, renders himself in a different medium, so that playing with forms means simultaneously being played by them' (Bollas 1993, p.41). Aesthetic experience and psychological transformation are thus intimately linked.

In both Winnicott's and Bollas' accounts a satisfactory maternal provision in infancy is the pre-condition for the adult equivalent in aesthetic response. On the other hand, both acknowledge that artwork of great value to others may be created in what is an attempt to repair psychic damage that is, for the artist concerned, an ultimate failure. While not doubting that the potential for aesthetic experience can be damaged in an individual, I would question whether this original infantile prototype, and of course its rehearsal in the adult therapeutic situation, is influential in such a necessary or straightforward way. It is as difficult to explain why some people seem to be imaginatively or aesthetically numb as it is to explain why some people become – or perhaps we should say remain – artists. Part of the psychoanalytic project is to to account for such phenomena in terms of formative infantile experiences; but outside a clinical context it is perhaps of less importance why they exist than how they operate.

There have also been some interesting accounts of the nature of aesthetic experience and its psychological lining, and the way these short-circuit the usual models of communication that come from outside the psychoanalytic sphere. Gaston Bachelard (1969), a pioneer in the investigation of the creative reception of literature, famously asserted that '... the image has touched the depths before it stirs the surface' (p.xix). He meant that we do not need to know the context from which it originates, nor to have shared the poet's suffering, in order for an immediate response to a poetic image to make itself felt. He calls this direct connection with depth 'reverberation', as opposed to the 'resonance' that characterises the horizontal network of associations and background information.

The question is, how far can Bachelard's phenomenological analyses, which are centered on language and the word, be applied to painting? Certainly one can imagine an anthology of similar responses to figurative art. In fact several such anthologies exist. But just as Bachelard seldom comments on the linguistic texture of his quotations, so such figurative or thematic reactions may be lured into a chain of associations that run the risk of overlooking the painting's material, aesthetic features. This is a common mode of response to representational works, one in which interest in the figurative content eclipses attention to its formal aspects. What is needed instead is a way of elaborating our response to a painting that enables us to shift backwards and forwards between the work's actual formal properties and its figurative reverberations, so that they influence one another reciprocally. Figurative excursions that start off from a creative and imaginative rather than a traditionally iconographic basis can be as much ways of articulating the aesthetic features of a work (its character of line, nuances of colour, textural variations and so on) as they are ways of exploring its narrative or symbolic meaning. This interaction between phantasy and the aesthetic is actually mutual: just as phantasy can serve to give a specific cast to a work's material facture, so these formal elements in turn can give a specific inflection to its figurative sense (this figure, painted this way). This is something I shall return to in Chapter Eight.

Endnotes

1. Cézanne is one of the painters to whom Merleau-Ponty devotes a great deal of attention (see his 'Cézanne's doubt' in Johnson 1993).
2. When Kandinsky saw these paintings in 1895 and for a moment failed to recognise their subject matter, he realised that the representational alibi could be dispensed with and a purely abstract painting was possible.
3. In art therapy it is fascinating how often an apparently practical remark ('the blue wouldn't stay put') has psychological undertones.
4. This was certainly Anton Ehrenzweig's explanation for the hostility generated in response to certain types of seemingly 'meaningless' abstract works of art (see Chapter Four).

Chapter Three

From Iconography to Embodiment

Suppose that all forms are, while they are perceived as pure form by the mind-body, simultaneously perceived and enjoyed as images by the body-mind ... I do not mean that the body translates form, abstractly perceived, into pictures; rather, that all form addresses itself no less to the body than the mind, the former perceiving it by virtue of its own formalizing tendencies and uniting with it. The body mates with forms no less than the mind does (Sewell 1971, p.38).

The above quotation is an unusual way of reminding us that perception involves an intimate partnership between mind and body: indeed, by talking about a 'mind-body' and a 'body-mind', Elisabeth Sewell questions our habitual distinction between the two. Yet aesthetic experience is often presented as being essentially disembodied or ethereal. This is partly because, as we saw in Chapter One, the relationship between the intellectual or 'formal' appreciation of art and its sensuous apprehension has often been an uneasy one. Some texts relate aesthetic enjoyment to a pure pleasure in looking, sometimes called 'scopophilia' by psychoanalysists. This pleasure is perhaps not so 'pure', because it involves fantasies of possession or penetration that have a voyeuristic tinge to them although they depend on an actual detachment from whatever scenes or objects are being (re)presented for the viewer's delectation.

There is no doubt that some paintings do seem to collude with this visual, or 'spectacular' appetite. Erotic, or eroticised, subjects are obvious examples. In his book *The Power of Images*, David Freedberg (1989) rightly criticises conventional, disembodied notions of aesthetic experience, and goes on to point out that our response to depictions of the body is much more highly charged. Unfortunately, he overstates his case:

When ... we find ourselves responding to an image of it as if it were real, it seems at that moment no mere signifier, but the living signified itself. Then, once the body is perceived as real and living, we are also capable of being roused by it ... there is a cognitive relation between looking and enlivening;

and between looking hard, not turning away, concentrating, and enjoying on the one hand, and possession and arousal on the other (p.325).

But there are many other, less erotic, instances of the pleasure afforded by looking.

For example, even seventeenth century Dutch still-lives play not only on the pictorial celebration of possession but also on the parallel material properties of the very painting that displays them. A good deal of post-modern aesthetic theorising has concentrated on the 'gaze' and its latent gender politics.[1] But however much such theory invokes psychoanalytic (or Lacanian) notions of bodily desire and phantasy, its effect is often to reinforce the displaced or postponed nature of the contribution such factors make to aesthetic response.

My point is, not that such analyses are of no use, but that their formal or iconographic emphasis is sometimes at the expense of more embodied aspects of aesthetic response. By 'embodied' I do not mean responses that are simply sexual, but ones that involve the body at a number of interacting levels. These include the 'reciprocity' and the sensorial leakages mentioned in the last chapter, but they also involve complex exchanges between our response to the material aesthetic qualities of a painting and responses that are both physical (such as 'gut reactions') and psychological (in the form of phantasies about the physical).

Aesthetic experience involves a much more complex psychosomatic texture than can be accounted for in terms of the detached or disembodied contemplation of formal properties. Yet the idea has persisted that aesthetic qualities are merely a surface allure, or that they are pre-eminently a matter of visual (or as Duchamp scathingly referred to it, 'retinal') apprehension. The way in which we conceive of aesthetic experience makes an enormous difference to the kind of psychological significance we expect to find in it, and to how we envisage the connection between the two. If we see aesthetic qualities in painting largely in terms of visual pleasure, or of purely formal considerations, then their psychological resonances will be correspondingly superficial; a different, more embodied viewpoint, on the other hand, will allow for a richer and deeper range of response.

Iconography: conscious and unconscious

We have already seen how Freud viewed a painting's aesthetic aspects as a kind of bribe or 'incitement premium' (Freud 1908). Clearly, he believed that the material or formal elements of art – line, colour, texture and so on – had no value in themselves, or rather, were in their unrefined form, dangerously close to the pleasure principle and primary process thinking. In a famous passage in a letter of 1914, he refers to a visit to the studio of some avant-garde artist: 'Meaning is but little to these men; all they care for is line, shape, agreement of contours. They are given up to the Lustprinzip [pleasure principle]' (quoted Spector 1972, p. 106). Evidently Freud assumed that this raw material had to be processed and refined both through the application of the artist's effort and skill and through proper obedience to the canons and conventions of representational art before it could have any real meaning.

These representational conventions are in fact intimately built into the structure of Freud's own theories about the translation of unconscious thoughts into pictorial form. Two concepts that are fundamental to such translation, namely the 'pictorialisation of thought' and the 'conditions of representability' in dreams, are evidently shaped by the artistic conventions of post-Renaissance art. Likewise, most of the processes of condensation, displacement, substitution and so forth that make up the 'dream-work' which is an intermediary stage between the unconscious ('latent') origins of a dream and its conscious ('manifest') recollection, are derived from the store of figurative devices with which we are familiar from art history. The point here is that Freud's use of these devices amounts to an iconography of the unconscious.

Furthermore, the interpretative method based upon it can be seen not only as a process of 'reading' the subtext behind dream imagery, but as a form of 'writing' that text in terms of unconscious symbolism. In either case, the aesthetic qualities of a painting (its 'how') are disregarded in favour of its underlying content (its 'what'). Etymologically, 'icono-graphy' means a writing with images, and all iconography, with the possible exception of geometric symbolism, is for this reason figurative.

It is hard to realise just how pervasive this figurative idiom is: it informs much of our picture of the inner life, not just of dream, but of phantasy and imagination. It also governs the ways in which they are supposed to be represented in art. Indeed there is a complex feedback loop between these representations and what might be thought of as the original or constitutive level of imagination. We often assume that works of art simply represent to us images and processes from our inner worlds, or that they give form and shape to what was previously indistinct. But we also absorb and adopt images that we encounter in the world of art. They become part of our imaginary vocabulary and then play their part in a kind of fantastic reproduction of themselves (Maclagan 1989a).

It is hardly surprising, then, that not only are psychoanalytic models of inner mental life predicated on this figurative mode, but that most of the interpretative language of therapy is still couched in this idiom. Such a figurative language involves not only 'scenes', 'part-objects' or 'figures', but also the narratives constructed around them, whether these are thought of as memory or as phantasy. Scenes and narratives also generate figurative iconographies.

It might be objected that this is not something peculiar to psychoanalysis, but is an inevitable by-product of the evolution and history of language. As Kafka (1994) said: 'For everything outside the phenomenal world language can only be used allusively, but never even approximately by way of comparison, since, corresponding as it does to the phenomenal world, it is concerned only with property and its relations' (p.14).

Kafka's comment could be seen as resignation to the fallen state of language: certainly it implies that its figurative use is problematic and open to misinterpretation. Yet for several centuries since the Renaissance it seemed plausible that the visual arts could develop a figurative pictorial 'language' that would not only serve to represent the external world, but would depict an inner, otherwise invisible world of dream, phantasy or vision. At the same time it would also provide the means for conveying, in symbolic objects or allegorical narratives, metaphysical themes (philosophical, moral or religious, for example).

The rise of Modernism has been associated with the erosion or collapse of this pictorial language. Nevertheless, there are still some areas of experience, including less articulate and more psychosomatic ones, which may escape this figurative net, but which could to some extent be caught in certain kinds of painting – particularly, of course, the non-figurative.

Another way of putting what I am trying to suggest is that there is an intimate dependence between the two senses of 'figurative' that seem at first to be so opposite: that which functions as a representation and that which functions non-literally or at a symbolic level. In effect, if we look at the history of post-Renaissance art, we can see that the 'proper' handling of the second depends upon the conventional legibility of the first. The repertoire of emblematic, allegorical or otherwise conventionally symbolic images that forms the basis of any iconography is inevitably bound up with a complex cluster of rules about figurative representation. Freud's 'conditions of representability' thus have a considerable, and unacknowledged, art-historical ancestry.

This enables us to understand why, in his scheme, different mental processes are associated with quite different modes of presentation. What Freud called 'primary process thinking', which operated at an unconscious level of the mind, more closely associated with the wish-fulfilling pressures of the pleasure principle, was characterised by a kind of opportunism and flexibility that was independent of any of the causal or logical processes associated with conscious rationality. It is, in effect, the peculiar character of this primary process that compels analysis to follow such devious paths of connection and to resort to such implausible forms of explanation (see for example, Spence 1987, pp. 128–9).

The relevance of this to non-representational art, or to art whose formal structure is in some way 'inarticulate' (a term we shall encounter in the next chapter) hinges on what might, paradoxically, be called the 'structure of unintelligibility'. Donald Kuspit (1993) has claimed that:

> In working our way through an abstract work of art we seem to be feeling our way in the labyrinth of preconscious and unconscious world of feelings. It is a highly ambivalent sensation, at once all too chaotic and exalted for Enlightenment reason. Such chaos and exaltation are at the core of primary process thinking (p. 117).

This unintelligible or 'inarticulate' character, that is in all sorts of ways, from the seductive to the aggressive, such a feature of modern art, is precisely what cannot be assimilated by Freud's approach, which both depends on and reinforces an 'iconographic prejudice' (Maclagan 1983, p. 10).

It has to be said that Jung's approach to pictorial imagery, at least in a therapeutic context, is, in its own way, equally iconographic. This is all the more surprising since Jung was a talented artist and painted images formed an important part of his own psychic exploration. On the strength of his own experience he went on to pioneer the use of painting and drawing as therapeutic aids (see Chapter Six). As we saw in Chapter One, Jung, too, disparaged the aesthetic aspects of art, identifying them with a narcissistic and irresponsible hedonism.

When we look at the documented ways in which he seems to have worked with his patient's images, it is clear that his interpretations are in terms of another, this time archetypal, symbolic vocabulary, and that aesthetic features such as changes of form and variations of colour are rarely touched on (Jung 1959, pp. 290–355). Indeed the Jungian tradition of handling such images has actually, in my view, got further to travel in this respect than the Freudian.

The doodle: a non-iconographic form

A glimpse into the cultural-historical context of these blind spots is provided by the history of the scribble, and more especially, of the doodle. In the early years of this century the term 'scribble' covered a wide range of informal and non-representational drawings. By definition, most of these were regarded as of no significance and were given little attention. The three areas where they did figure were in child art, in mediumnistic drawings and in psychotic art. Of these three, psychotic art represents the most dramatic lapse, or collapse, from conventional standards of representation or symbolisation.

In Prinzhorn's (1972) comprehensive survey *Artistry of the Mentally Ill*, referred to in Chapter One, 'disorganised, aimless scribbling' is put forward as the most primitive manifestation of 'the configurative urge' (p.14). But the plates illustrating typical 'scribbles' actually include a number of drawings that, while not representing anything, are nonetheless quite structured. They are works that today would be seen and accepted as 'abstract' art.

The principal category within which Prinzhorn made sense of these informal drawings was that of 'decoration or ornament'. In 'schizophrenic' art these tendencies were elaborated in such an exaggerated form that they burst out of the conventional limits assigned to them. There is a fascinating issue here, about what Western art has obscured under the blanket of the ornamental: one that Worringer (1953) took the first steps in addressing in his influential *Abstraction and Empathy* (first published 1908).

But there was also another possibility: that such non-representational works might parallel the efforts of 'serious' avant-garde art. Here there was 'a renunciation of the outside world as commonly understood, as well as a logical devaluation of the surface luster upon which all Western art has heretofore depended, and finally a decisive turn inward upon the self' (Prinzhorn 1972, p.272).

We can see clearly here how such work, with its inevitable concentration on purely 'formal' features, seems to lack the natural advantage of the figurative tradition, and how for Prinzhorn the ambition to achieve an art that 'should deal only with pure psychic qualities' was an 'extravagant, grandiose, often compulsively distorted' one (1972, p.272). By the end of his remarkable study, Prinzhorn was forced to admit that there was no way of distinguishing by stylistic features alone the difference between a 'schizophrenic' work from one created by a modern artist, since both sought to convey such 'pure psychic qualities'.

In a similar way the popular cult of the 'doodle', which seems to have begun in the mid 1920s, centres on attempts to give interpretations – half graphological, half psychoanalytic – of typically marginal, absent-minded drawings. These readings were usually in terms of primitive stylistic features such as the preponderance of lines or curves, or their more or less geometrical organisation. In other words, here too there is an attempt to make sense of formal, or what could be called aesthetic, features in terms of an elementary subliminal 'language', and to relate this to a kind of bowdlerised unconscious symbolism.

Strictly speaking, the language of doodles, because it occupies a liminal position between the representational, the decorative and the abstract, is almost beyond the reach of iconographic readings. Its graphological aspects, however, because of their kinesic influences (for example, most left-handed doodles are structurally different from right-handed ones) are much closer to aesthetic qualities that are embodied. It is fascinating to see how these non-representational doodles were widely accepted as a kind of unconscious lingua franca, while contemporary Modernist experiments in art of a not dissimilar kind were regarded with suspicion or ridicule.

All of this does something to suggest the difficulties that early psychiatry and psychoanalysis had to overcome in order to begin to arrive at a more sophisticated psychological understanding of those 'aesthetic' features that were to be found in relatively unadulterated form in both doodles and abstract art. In the period between the two wars, many psychiatrists rashly published studies of such avant-garde artists as Cézanne or Kandinsky, in which they brandished diagnoses of 'schizoid tendencies' or even outright psychosis on the basis of the distortions of representation or loss of contact with external reality to be found in their works. Even Jung, in his essay on Picasso, classes the artist's work in the category 'schizophrenic' because of its fragmentation and supposed lack of feeling. Perhaps it would be fair to see this as a characterisation of its general psychological style, rather than as a psychiatric diagnosis of the artist, although Jung clearly felt Picasso to be at some personal risk (Jung 1984, originally published 1934).

Abstraction and the inner world: in or beyond the body?

In all of these attempts to make psychological sense of the hyper-expressive or non-representational aspects of Modernism – or more often, to refuse to do so – there is a common thread: that of the problems raised by the fracture or collapse of traditional conventions of representation. This phenomenon has, of course, many contemporary parallels in such diverse fields as literature, music, and even philosophy or physics. The crisis of representation in art is linked to an emphatic shift in focus, from outer to 'inner' reality; and since there is no equivalent to the previous consensus on figurative conventions for the expression of such an inner reality, the actual aesthetic handling of a painting – its marks, colours and compositional sub-groupings – has to carry an increasing weight. In many ways this shift operates irrespective of whether the artistic programme in question is, for example, Futuristic or Constructivist.[2]

There was, of course, a wide variety of different inflections in Modernism of the aim to depict inner or psychological reality in ways that were, as far as is possible, uncontaminated with external associations.

At one end of the spectrum is Kandinsky's notion of 'inner necessity' and its connection with 'the nonmaterial strivings and searchings of the thirsty soul' (Kandinsky, quoted Harrison 1996, p.141). These ambitions were often expressed in terms of an 'utterly spiritualised and dematerialised inwardness of feeling' (Marc 1910, quoted in Harrison 1996, p.144). Such strivings were eminently compatible with more traditional attitudes towards aesthetic qualities which, as we have seen, were supposed to be suitably remote from any down-to-earth or material involvement; later on I shall contrast this view of aesthetic experience with a more embodied one. But there were other strands in Modernism, such as Zurich Dadaism, that emphasised natural and immediate forms of expression that would not be so distant from the body.

Sublimation: the translation of bodily experience into paint

Contemporary psychoanalysis was, of course, suspicious of any claim, religious or artistic, to transcend the body and its desires. Psychoanalytic theory did establish one way in which embodiment was intimately related to the material handling of paint or clay: this was in terms of one of Freud's pre-genital developmental stages, that of anality. There are obvious reasons for the symbolic and cultural functions of anality: not only does the anus function, symbolically as well as literally, as a key site of passage from inside to outside, but its excretory products are given opposite values by the infant and its caretakers. Notoriously, children play with their faeces and treat them as precious gifts to adults, who in contrast find them disgusting. According to Freud, the achievement of toilet-training, like weaning before it, entails the surrender of one realm of uninhibited bodily gratification in exchange for a sense of mastery and the satisfactions offered by progression to the next stage. The repressed bodily satisfactions are then translated into unconscious phantasy.

Faeces certainly do evoke a whole experiential spectrum, from the sloppy to the compact, from control and retention to explosive incontinence; and each of these has its own metaphoric resonance. Paint, by its very consistency, as well as in the activities associated with it of squeezing, smearing, dribbling and so on, lends itself to perform as a phantastic analogue for these body products and how they might be 'handled', so to speak. There are also echoes, in the anxiety or disgust evoked in the artist by the messy results of the use of his materials, as well as in the guilty enjoyment of 'messing about', of the feelings once aroused in infancy about excreta.

References abound in the psychoanalytic literature to painting being deeply informed by anality. This is partly because the anal is, on account of its adult association with disgust, the object par excellence of sublimation. If Freud himself did not directly link painting with anality, then his followers did so eagerly. The possibility of the activity of painting per se being a sublimation of anal gratification enabled psychoanalysis to extend its hermeneutic grip over the whole of art, rather than just over those works that might be seen to be 'symbolic' depictions of sexual scenes or organs (see Gay 1992, pp.36–7).

The danger of using anality as a kind of sublimatory 'open-sesame' is that it is both reductive (painting is nothing more than sophisticated shit-playing) and indiscriminate (aren't some kinds of slippery, squidgy facture more interesting than others?). Howard Gardner (1973) has suggested that Freud's developmental stages can be treated as 'modes' of experience, in which bodily functions have a gradually developing metaphoric resonance:

> [The child] becomes increasingly able to transfer these modal experiences, which occur initially within his body, or in relation to objects in contact with his body, to the perception and making of objects external to himself.[...] The modes and vectors become a set of categories that he can bring to bear on the full range of his experience; in addition, they come to combine with one another in diverse ways, giving rise to distinct emotions, styles, aesthetic categories, and temperamental strains (p.102).

This perspective treats bodily experience as always having what I called earlier a 'psychological lining', and allows sublimation to be more of a developing process than just an adult symbolic transaction.

The traditional Freudian notion of sublimation is riddled with problems: how is sexualised energy diverted to non-sexual aims such as intellectual or artistic achievement; how much of the instinctual source (sexual, oral, anal or whatever) still colours the supposedly de-sexualised psychic energy used for this; and are some forms of sublimation 'better' (more efficient, of higher value) than others? There are also questions about what factors – psychological, educational, cultural – enable or inhibit sublimation (Maclagan 1999).

Painting seems, in comparison with purely intellectual activity, a less abstract or disembodied form of sublimation. Indeed it may well be that certain kinds of art – particularly those with a 'raw' facture or 'primitive' imagery – have what could be called a 'desublimatory' effect, in that they return the sophistication of art back towards what Bakhtin called 'the lower bodily strata', and that this would be connected with their aesthetic properties. One example of this might be some of Francis Bacon's paintings where thickly smeared and heavily churned passages of paint suggestive of coupling figures are set off against lush velvety backgrounds of impeccably brushed colour.

Object-relations: towards a non-figurative aesthetic

With the emergence of 'object relations', under the influence of Melanie Klein's theories, psychoanalysis begins to elaborate a framework within which psychological conflicts are enacted in terms of bodily states and processes. These can be connected to non-figurative features of painting. Early object-relations did, of course, have its own equivalents for Freudian symbols: 'good' and 'bad' breasts and other 'part-objects' (penises, faeces, babies and so on); but these are involved in complex exchanges (for example, in phantasy where faeces are equated with a penis or with babies; or urine can symbolise seminal potency or poisonous attack). Thus in Klein's (1986) own writings infantile phantasies centering on somatic processes and the exchange of bodily products play a more dynamic role and their symbolic functions are highly flexible.

The importance of this is manifold. First, psychoanalysis is now in a position to offer a psychological understanding of the disposition of the formal or aesthetic features of a work of art, such as the balance between 'order' or conventional 'beauty' as against 'disorder' or 'ugliness'; and second, the bodily idiom in which these conflicts are rehearsed is more 'internal' and process-oriented (for example in terms of the phantasied incorporation or expulsion of good or bad part-objects). It is true that object-relations can still be used to construct an iconographic vocabulary of part-objects,[3] but it can also be used in a more sophisticated way, to deal with overall compositional tensions, as well as with particular passages of facture within a work of art. Indeed the work's final structure can be seen as carrying within it 'souvenirs' of the psychological conflicts of which it is a temporary resolution (Segal 1992).

A particularly interesting crossover between the world of object-relations and that of art criticism is to be found in the writings of Adrian Stokes, who was also a painter. Throughout his writing he evokes a dynamic interplay in our relationship to the artwork between the two poles of envelopment and separation, the latter represented both by the depiction of distinctly defined objects and, ultimately, by the artwork's own concrete existence independent of the spectator. These correspond to early infantile experiences of proximity to the breast and a sense of separation from it (associated with what Klein called the 'depressive position'):

> There is, then, in art a firm alliance between generality and the obdurate otherness of objects, as if an alliance, in regard to the body, between the positive rhythmic experiences of the infant at the breast and the subsequent appreciation of the whole mother's separate existence (also internalised), complete to herself, uninjured by his aggressive or appropriating fantasies...
> (Stokes 1972, p.118)

But what makes Stokes different from most other writers adopting an object-relations perspective is the way he allows the metaphoric resonance of such infantile bodily fantasies to expand:

> Rembrandt, it seems to me, painted the female nude as the sagging repository of jewels and dirt, of fabulous babies and magical faeces despoiled yet later repaired and restored, a body often flaccid and creased yet still the desirable source of a scarred bounty: not the bounty of the perfected, stable breast housed in the temple of the integrated psyche that we possess in the rounded forms of classical art, but riches and drabness joined by the infant's interfering envy, sometimes with the character of an oppressive weight or listlessness left by his thefts. There supervenes, none the less, a noble acceptance of ambivalence in which love shines (Stokes 1972, p.119).

What is at work here is a creative and poetic 'performance' of Rembrandt's nudes of the sort that I shall have more to say about in Chapter Eight.

Stokes also raises the possibility that certain kinds of expressionist or abstract painting can evoke such bodily fantasies in a more diffuse way:

> ... we possess in some abstract art an intense figuration for the concourse of corporeal inner objects ... though divorced in this case from the significance of their attachment to precise and self-subsistent models from the outside world; and it may well be that in common with most image-making, exaggeration and distortion in modern representational art has proceeded less from aggression than from the need to describe inner states as far as possible as such, in an outer form (Stokes 1978, p.11).

This will also be relevant, as we shall see, to the example of the conflicting understandings of the 'attack' to be seen in De Kooning's 'Women' paintings (Chapter Eight). The wider question, implicit here, is whether all modalities of imagination in and about the body, and their sublimation into painting, have to be subsumed under the category of early infantile phantasy.

I want to suggest that there is a whole domain of what could be called unconscious bodily or embodied phantasy that includes what psychoanalysis proposes and extends beyond it. Such fantasies are not just of the body or its parts as 'seen' externally (such as might occur in visualisations or dreams), but of the body or its parts as 'felt' from the inside. By this I mean more than the ordinary proprioception of body states such as blood pressure, muscular tension or of processes such as peristalsis (though there is no reason why these should not be a part of the kinesthetic repertoire of painting).

There is also a whole dimension of less realistic body phantasy, that deals with the imagination of these processes irrespective of their actual functioning. There are well-known examples of this excessive phantasy life in popular culture such as comic strips and animated films.[4] These form something like the riotous, anarchic obverse of more scientifically correct images of the body, or educational visual metaphors such as the digestive system pictured as an assembly line.

Some paintings depict this body imagery more or less directly: much of Masson's work, or early Rothkos and late Gorkys, for example, deal in a kind of 'organic' form that has plausible, more or less specific, relations to body parts or organs.[5] Tanguy and Matta, on the other hand, could be said to deal with 'inscapes' that suggest more diffuse or indeterminate anatomical landscapes. However this perspective could be taken even further, to include the actual facture of some paintings: their brushwork, colouring and formal dynamics. In the case of De Kooning, for example, it could be argued that there is a kind of double figuration: at one level in his subject matter (most obviously in his women), and at another level in the elisions and juxtapositions of his very brushstrokes.[6]

In all of these instances we are dealing with connections between large scale structural elements or the local detail of painterly form (what we shall see Enhrenzweig call 'inarticulate form' in the next chapter) and a variety of more or less coherent imaginary reflections or manipulative fantasies to do with the body, its parts or functions. As I have already said, these do not all have to be herded into the corral of psychoanalytic unconscious symbolism: they may operate at any level, from the conscious to the subliminal to the very edge of experience beyond which things are unconscious.[7]

Some Klein-influenced writers on art were still suspicious of such slippery forms. Adrian Stokes was certainly ambivalent about painting that strayed too close to unalloyed Primary Process. Writing about an unspecified kind of abstract art (perhaps not unlike de Kooning) he says: 'We have here the manner of endless bodily function as well as of hardly touched states of mind, more muscular, more independent than the resonance of images in a dream, yet, when viewed in terms of the intellect's categories, vague and boundless as are the spongy images of sleep...' (Stokes 1972, p.82).

The danger of being swallowed up in such inchoate form has to be countered, according to Stokes, by a compositional structure or 'architecture'. However, he also allows for the possibility that the sheer physical other-ness of the artwork may itself provide such an antidote:

> ... we are shown an aspect of our environment and 'mental climate' by the painter as an enclosed object, at arm's length, reflecting what I have called two basic relationships to objects. They are usually experienced together; in art alone their collusion seems perfected to the extent that we appear to have the

cake and eat it without a greedy tearing, the object to incorporate and the object set out and self-contained (Stokes 1972, p.90).

There are fascinating glimpses here of an oral, rather than just an anal, mode of relating to art.[8]

How are we to take up these bodily metaphors from object-relations in relation to aesthetic features and their psychological reverberations? If we apply them reductively, we end up infantilising the artist, and art, and the significance yielded is at a primitive level. As I have suggested, the whole Freudian concept of sublimation needs to be re-thought in terms of the imaginative elaboration of bodily experience. As Malcolm Bowie (1993) points out in relation to Freud:

> The opportunities are legion for a psychoanalytically informed criticism to avoid oscillating simplistically between the complete art work on the one hand and the hypothetical early events that 'explain' it on the other, to observe passion at work upon paint, or stone, or language, or musical sound, and to see the drives of the artist shaping and being shaped by the materials to hand (p.57).

My contention has been that these profound bodily metaphors play a much richer and more sophisticated role, both in painting and in aesthetic response, than is usually allowed for. Indeed their situation within psychoanalytic theory, even at a clinical level, let alone an applied or cultural one (and the two are not really distinct), is a special form of comprehension, or rather, capture. This has more to do with the need of analysis to establish a biological, or quasi-biological, foundation for its speculative and theoretical constructions than with the more complex connections between aesthetic and psychological in painting that are the focus of this book.

The dynamic balance in a work of art, between formal properties such as coherence and incoherence, and between psychological factors such as creative and destructive impulses, plays a crucial role in Anton Ehrenzweig's theories about the unconscious substructure of art. While Ehrenzweig made use of the conceptual apparatus of object-relations, he introduced major revisions to the Freudian model of the unconscious psyche and its processes. In fact, as Jean-François Lyotard has pointed out, in his thinking it is no longer a matter of psychoanalysis being 'applied' to art, but of certain key features of art having a radical impact on psychoanalytic theory itself (Lyotard 1983).

Endnotes

1. Griselda Pollock (1996) has skillfully engineered a feminist reversal of the privileged masculine gaze in Manet's Bar at the Folies Bergères.

2. Futurism itself, despite its machismo, displayed spiritualistic inclinations (for example in some of Carra and Balla's paintings).

3. A somewhat extreme example is the research embarked on by the analyst Dr Grace Pailthorpe in 1935, with the assistance of the artist Reuben Mednikoff, to 'use art as a short cut to the deeper levels of the unconscious'. Many of the pictures they produced literally reproduce the phantasy world of early infancy (and even intra-uterine experiences), peopled with animated part-objects (see Maclagan 1998).

4. Early Walt Disney animation is an excellent example of how body parts can be depicted as stretching, compressing and rebounding in every conceivable fashion.

5. There is considerable debate as to how far Gorky's late paintings are, or are not, disguised forms of figuration. Some critics contend that there is a detectable figurative basis to all of them (Rand 1981), while others talk in more metaphorical or analogical terms.

6. This has been dealt with, in very different ways by Kuspit (1998) and Schiff (1994). See Chapter Eight.

7. Modern psychoanalytic thought, especially under the influence of Lacan, would concede that unconscious processes can never be accessed directly, but only at one or more removes.

8. Such metaphors are more readily applicable to reading, where books are 'devoured' or found 'hard to digest'. But Stokes has some prescient pages on the oral greed underlying looking that is often enhanced by painting (Stokes 1972, p.90).

Chapter Four

From Inarticulate to Aesthetic Form

The psychoanalytic concept of creative sublimation implies that the highest
human achievement should be linked very directly with what is lowest and
most primitive in ourselves [...] Psychoanalysis does not drag the sublime
through the mud by making such connections. On the contrary; once we have
accepted the dynamic model of creative sublimation which psychoanalysis has
introduced, we can only expect that the most sublime be joined by a
short-circuit with what is most debased in human nature. Nothing else will do,
and squeamish readers who cannot bear such juxtapositions should keep away
from depth-psychology (Ehrenzweig 1967, pp.128–9).

Anton Ehrenzweig's ideas make revolutionary links between the psychology of
perception, in its respectable Gestalt form, and the psychoanalytic model of
consciousness under the powerful influence of unconscious processes. Yet
despite enjoying a certain popularity at the time, his ideas have subsequently
fallen into a strange kind of limbo: his name is often absent from books in the
field of psychoanalysis and art that should at least refer to him, and he has
become something of an eminence grise.[1]

Ehrenzweig's notion of a 'depth mind' that operates according to
form-principles foreign to the conscious mind, but which also offers structures
which are richer and more complex than rational ones, effectively inverts the
conventional relationship between art and psychoanalysis, giving art the lead.
It is perhaps for this reason that, in my experience, Ehrenzweig's writings have
a real appeal for artists: they recognise that he has a genuine understanding of
art and a proper appreciation of its contribution to a properly psychological
aesthetics.

Ehrenzweig was not just a psychoanalytic theoretician: he had himself
undergone a seven-year analysis in Vienna before the Anschluss made him a
refugee in Britain (Tony Ehrenzweig, personal communication), and he was
also a musician and painter. Furthermore, he ended up as an art teacher at Goldsmith's College, London where his controversial methods had a considerable
impact on individual students.[2] His last book, *The Hidden Order of Art* (1967),

published the year after his death, made an important contribution to the innovatory climate of art education in the early 1970s. One reason for the widespread effect of what is in many ways a complicated and compressed book is Ehrenzweig's unashamed championing of the modern artist as a serious investigator of unconscious phenomena, and his remarkable analyses of the complex formal structures of artworks.

A few sentences from the preface to the second edition of his first book, *The Psychoanalysis of Artistic Vision and Hearing* (1975, first published 1953) show the extent of Ehrenzweig's claims on behalf of modern painting: 'It was thought that the structure of unconscious processes was unstructured and even totally chaotic. The evidence of artistic production proves otherwise. Art's substructure is shaped by deeply unconscious processes and may display a complex organisation that is superior to the logical structure of conscious thought' (Ehrenzweig 1975, p.viii). This unconscious substructure forms the basis for a new psychoanalytic aesthetics: it is in this first book that Ehrenzweig gave the most accessible account of what he called 'inarticulate' or 'Gestalt-free' form and of its subliminal effects.

Inarticulate form and aesthetic revision

'Inarticulate form' is a highly ambiguous and multivalent type of form, whose structure (or apparent lack of it) defies the laws of Gestalt perception, in that there is no longer any significant 'figure' to set, with any reliability, against a 'ground'.[3] Because it eludes the Gestalt net in which the conscious mind captures phenomena inarticulate form is thus 'structurally' unconscious, hence it is associated with a differently constituted 'depth mind'.

> ...when we turn our eye inwards, as in play, art, day-dreaming, or in the deep dreams of our sleep, and the mental energy is drained from the surface of the mind into its depth, then our vision loses its sharp and well-defined edge, the forms perceived become more fluid and intermingle and separate in a continuous flux (Ehrenzweig 1975, p.30).

Thus vagueness, fluidity and superimposition are the characteristics of inarticulate form, and they seem to have much in common with the compressed, illogical idiom of Freud's 'primary process thinking' (although as we shall see, this is not actually the case).

Inarticulate form plays an important part in a great many different kinds of human mental function: not only in perception, but even in creative intellectual or scientific work, as well as in dreaming or art-making. Just as the antecedents of the train of thought we are now aware of are effectively eclipsed in the process of our becoming conscious of it, so the contributions of inarticulate form to the process of seeing are also effectively invisible in the final results of perception that reach consciousness. Although Ehrenzweig begins by describing inarticulate form in mainly 'structural' terms, it does, as we shall see, have important psychological resonances, particularly when it is foregrounded in certain kinds of art.

In fact, inarticulate form plays a part in almost all kinds of painting or drawing[4], even though its presence may be literally a 'background' one. It is present in the absent-mindedly sketched-in secondary or background forms of traditional art that are created in an 'automatic' or diffuse state of conscious-ness, and which give the work its inimitable feel of liveliness. Conscious attempts to copy such spontaneous and un-thought forms, as in traditional academic transcriptions, are unable to recreate this feel.

What occurs in a marginal way in such conventional work becomes a much more central feature of modern art:

> The modern artist tends to create more automatically, with less conscious form control, than the traditional artist. At the beginning he knows only vaguely, if at all, what he is going to produce; his mind is curiously empty while he watches passively the forms growing from under his brush. Automatic form control means that the depth mind has taken over the form production which therefore now reflects the gestalt-free structure of the depth mind. Hence, the lack of a pregnant eye-catching pattern, the superimposition, overlapping, and general ambiguity of forms which could never be achieved by conscious form control (Ehrenzweig 1975, p.33).

Ehrenzweig calls this relaxation of conscious control 'de-differentiation': in it normal discriminations between one form and another, or even between self and not-self, are suspended, and a more inclusive kind of 'vision' comes into play. Hence the capacity to handle undifferentiated form plays a crucial role in creative innovation in many fields beside art.

Not only does this depend on the artist's capacity to tolerate fragmentary and irrational elements, but it also entails a similar tolerance on the part of the spectator viewing the end-product. Indeed there is a rhythmic alternation in each case, between submergence in unconscious, inarticulate form and a more conscious level of appreciation and organisation. According to Ehrenzweig a similar process went on in the case of both dreams and jokes, which were the objects of Freud's original analyses of unconscious processes. In both cases what Freud puts forward as the unconscious mechanism at work (the dream-work and the parallel trains of thought that are knotted together in the joke's punchline) is in fact a secondary rationalisation of an original inarticulate level: 'What Freud calls primary process structures are merely distortions of articulate surface imagery caused by the underlying undifferentiation of truly unconscious phantasy' (Ehrenzweig 1967, p.263). We can already see here how Ehrenzweig's ideas entail a revision of classical psychoanalytic boundaries between conscious and 'unconscious' processes.

The conscious mind's resistance to assimilating inarticulate form is not just a perceptual difficulty: there is also a psychologically disconcerting aspect to it. There is something inherently threatening about its confusing and multivalent character, and a corresponding anxiety, with which most artists are familiar, about pictorial chaos descending into irretrievable mess. In Ehrenzweig's three-stage model of the creative process in art, this anxiety is succeeded by a 'manic-oceanic' phase, in which the artist feels so in tune with inarticulate form that everything in his artwork seems to hang together.

Similar reactions also occur in the spectator's reaction to the finished work, both as immediate response and as part of their imaginative recreation of the work. Ehrenzweig points out that this explains some of the hostility aroused by non-figurative work: 'Many people like their art mellowed and seasoned by the action of secondary processes and will therefore reject the raw modern art of their own period' (Ehrenzweig 1967, p.87). It is interesting to contrast Ehrenzweig's openness to primitive or experimental art forms with the more conservative attitude of Adrian Stokes (sampled in the last chapter). This 'seasoning' is, as we shall see, related to what Ehrenzweig sees as the function of 'aesthetic' improvements made to the work in its final stages.

Ehrenzweig attempted to distinguish 'between the structural repression inherent in unconscious form processes and the superego's repression directed against the archaic or infantile contents symbolised in them' (Ehrenzweig 1975, p.16); in other words, between repression of form and repression of content. However, there is also an important affinity between the loose, indeterminate structure of inarticulate form and phantasy that is unconscious in a strictly psychoanalytic sense: 'the ego supplies undifferentiated form exactly fitted to express the undifferentiated aims of the id' (Ehrenzweig 1975, p.269). The result is a latent and pervasive anxiety, a fear of being submerged in an undifferentiated matrix.

For Ehrenzweig this in itself was not enough to explain the almost inevitable pressure to subject inarticulate form to processes of secondary revision. This was also caused by the artist's conscious awareness that his work would eventually be submitted to an audience. In the third stage of the creative process, therefore, the artwork is subject to revisions, in which inarticulate form is modified by 'aesthetic' decisions. Hence, while the work's liveliness might be due to inarticulate form operating at a subliminal level, its apparent aesthetic quality was due to more conscious processes. It is easy to confuse the two, as we have seen in the case of Freud's theories about jokes and dreams, where the 'logic' of the dream-work that derives from secondary revision (condensation, displacement and so forth) is mistaken for the structure of unconscious process itself.

Ehrenzweig believed that this kind of digestion occurred in all aesthetic experience, both in the artist creating his work and in the spectator viewing it. In fact, this conscious assimilation was so automatic that it was experientially impossible to return to the original shocking impact of inarticulate form.[5] As an adjunct to this inevitable conscious process of smoothing over and tidying up, Ehrenzweig was led to invoke the traditional psychoanalytic impulse of 'anal disgust' as the principal motive behind the need to give a more rational organisation to the indiscriminate melée of inarticulate form. Here aesthetic pleasure functions as a compensation for the loss of unconscious gratification that is a result of this secondary revision (Ehrenzweig 1975, pp.61–3). But it is important to remember that this compensatory function is not simply a 'sweetener' to smooth the passage of unconscious imagery into consciousness, as in Freud. It is one side of a dynamic interplay between 'Dionysian' (depth, inarticulate) and 'Apollinian' (surface, gestalt) forms, so that 'the increase in aesthetic pleasure [is] not dependent on a real improvement in the gestalt properties of the surface gestalt, but quite the contrary, the plastic and aesthetic impression increase[s] the more surface gestalt [is] disintegrated by the competing form events' (Ehrenzweig 1975, p.60).

As we have seen, this secondary revision is associated with the shift from a 'manic-oceanic' enjoyment of (con)fusion, an ineffable comprehension that transcends all contradiction, to a 'depressive' position in which the artist detaches himself from his work, becomes a spectator to it, and judges it accordingly (Ehrenzweig 1967, pp.192–4). Similar processes presumably go on in a spectator confronted with a challenging or unconventional painting. They also occur on a larger, cultural scale when artistic innovations are gradually assimilated by the art world and are turned, in the end, into stylistic devices or mannerisms (Ehrenzweig 1967, pp.66–9).

The question, of course, is what gives these final revisions their 'aesthetic' character. Freud had suggested that our concept of 'beauty' is phylogenetically the result of an early shift from interest in and excitement by the strictly genital areas, which he believed were not beautiful, to a more diffuse attraction to other parts of the body or to the body as a whole.

However, as we saw in the last chapter, even the pleasure of looking is still coloured by desire in a way that is, for example, quite at odds with Kant's notion of the 'disinterestedness' which should be at the basis of aesthetic judgement (I shall have more to say about the passionate response to beauty in the next chapter).[6] Going even further than Freud, Ehrenzweig constructs a bizarre speculative prehistory of humanity to account for the special functions of anality in relation to beauty: 'Man's over development of the aesthetic sense, which is a precondition for his appreciation of the abstract Gestalt for its own sake, may be a dumb reaction formation to the flooding of perception with undifferentiated archaic (pan-genital, pan-anal) urges' (Ehrenzweig 1975, p.220).[7]

Both Freud's and Ehrenzweig's speculations are some of the more extreme instances of the need of psychoanalysis to give its theories of psychic function not only a biological but an historical authority (in this case almost a combination of the two), and it can be seen as one of many attempts to supply an alternative, supposedly non-metaphysical, grounding for aesthetics.[8]

The important thing, however, is not to set up an antagonism between instinctual pressures and their sublimation, but to preserve a dynamic and rhythmic interplay between depth and surface. For Ehrenzweig it is this that accounts for the sense of aliveness and depth in both perception and art, and that prevents aesthetic organisation from congealing into conventional 'standards' of beauty as, for example, it tended to do in eighteenth and nineteenth century academic art.

This is also what accounts both for the fact that artists are never satisfied by their work and for the way in which originally Dionysian form is transmuted into a more Apollinian style. These are terms taken over from Nietzsche's writing on Greek tragic drama, where the relation between Dionysian ecstatic excess and Apollonian order is one where the former is given an aesthetic transfiguration by the latter (Nietzsche 1956, pp.24–8).[9]

The psychological effects of engaging with inarticulate form

Ehrenzweig's dynamic picture of the relation between surface and depth also entails a new picture of the unconscious mind. As selected elements of undifferentiated form are brought up into consciousness, others will drop back and so enrich the store of unconscious material: 'Unconscious phantasy life during our whole lifetime is supplied with new imagery by the ego's cyclical rhythm of dedifferentiation, which feeds fresh material into the matrix of image-making' (Ehrenzweig 1967, p.263). An artist who engages in this vertical traffic to a more than ordinary extent might thus be expected to renovate his unconscious more than normal.

This helps to explain another of Ehrenzweig's remarkable claims on behalf of art: namely that the artist's intra-psychic dialogue with his work is an equivalent to the inter-psychic dialogue between patient and analyst. The artist's work acts as a 'receiving womb' in which initially fragmentary elements are integrated into a coherent whole by a process of unconscious scanning (the 'manic-oceanic' phase of the creative process) and finally is subject to more conscious organisation. As a by-product of this sequence, the artist's unconscious is enriched by the unconscious fall-out from the final phase (Ehrenzweig 1967, pp.104–5).

This relates to the idea, suggested in some of Marion Milner's writings (Milner 1987, pp.221–3), that the experience of art-making is in itself, quite apart from the psychological significance of its results, 'therapeutic'. The question then arises: does the artist alone qualify for this benefit because of his intimate psychic involvement in the precarious passages of the creative process, or can the spectator, if sufficiently able to pursue an internal engagement with the work, also qualify? I think that this would be a logical consequence of Ehrenzweig's theory, and I believe that this justifies the importance attached in this book to the psychological repercussions of aesthetic experience.

I think that there is also a parallel here with the effects of the 'literature' of psychoanalysis on readers as compared with the effects of its clinical application. It is often maintained that only those who have been in analysis can really 'know' psychoanalysis, and that this constitutes a crucial difference between analysis and 'psychoanalytic studies' (which would include its cultural applications).[10] However, while the effects of transference and other therapeutic phenomena are obviously more pronounced in actual face-to-face analysis, they are nonetheless also present in the reading of case studies and even of theoretical texts. Bollas' (1987) suggestions about the ways in which works of art can function as 'transformational objects' (pp.16–17) (touched on in Chapter Two) are relevant here. What is also interesting is that the implications of these ideas for art therapy have yet to be taken up (see Chapter Six).

Inarticulate form, spontaneity and unconscious creation

The need to reorganise inarticulate form in the final stages of creating a work of art does not, even according to Ehrenzweig's own criteria, have to be impelled by unconsciously prompted anxiety or anal disgust: it is simply the case that unconscious material, by definition, can never be made conscious in an unadulterated state. In this respect Ehrenzweig anticipated Lacan's distinction between the Symbolic Order and unconscious phenomena that lay outside it. As Ehrenzweig says, '…we cannot produce the originally undifferentiated structure of the primary process for conscious inspection, but only its conscious derivates like conglomerated, bizarre condensations, illogical displacements and the like' (Ehrenzweig 1967, p.268).

The question still remains, however, whether certain kinds of painting, of which Pollock's or De Kooning's are only the most obvious and celebrated examples, do not embody such structures in ways that are more direct?

Certainly Ehrenzweig was quick to see that these kinds of painting foregrounded inarticulate form in dramatic, if not confrontational, ways:

> The evolution from traditional art to modern art simply withdraws the bigger forms also from conscious control; so the vague and ambiguous forms of automatic form creation are no longer contained in the technique [facture] or in the misty forms of the background, but break out from their hide-out and invade the whole picture (Ehrenzweig 1975, p.34).

The psychological implications of this shift, from an art concerned with the depiction of external reality and therefore apparently investing in it libidinally, to an 'abstract' art that appears to withdraw from this reality, are not what they seem.

According to Ehrenzweig, the realism of post-Renaissance art is actually the expression of an investment in the technical forms of secondary revision, such perspective or proportion, rather than in the original fluctuating forms of thing-perception itself (Ehrenzweig 1975, p.255). What he calls 'abstract' art represents the culmination of this process: the libidinous loss which is so clearly marked in our 'abstract' (thing-free) art is also noticeable in science (Ehrenzweig 1975, p.256). Clearly he had in mind the kind of abstract art that allowed the artist to 'freely invent new forms that could express *ideas* in purely aesthetic terms' (Ehrenzweig 1967, p.146, my emphasis). This style, of which Constructivism is one example, had become such a tired recipe that he foresaw the need for new forms of abstraction that would seem a 'mess' by comparison.

However, not all abstract art fits this first model of detachment and disembodiment. I have already suggested that the inchoate facture of an 'abstract' De Kooning evokes subliminal bodily resonances that would certainly qualify as 'libidinal investment' (it is significant here that De Kooning insisted his painting was always figurative). In a different way, looking at a huge 'all-over' Pollock painting like No. 31, 1950 throws normal Gestalt-based modes of perception completely out of kilter, so that a swimming, 'oceanic' effect is produced, which also reproduces something of the transformed perception of things in mystical or ecstatic experience.

In such paintings (but also in the wildness hidden in the facture of a Bonnard or a Soutine, for example) inarticulate form seems to present something that is difficult to integrate both into the conventions of 'normal' perception and into those of semiotic or symbolic analysis. Its informal structure, with all its elisions and overlaps, cannot be sorted out into 'signs', or indeed even 'marks', on the basis of which a formal analysis could be essayed. It seems, therefore, to stand on the edge of the symbolic, to have a liminal, if not subliminal, status.

There is, however, a danger in identifying the unconscious substructure of art too closely with certain formal styles or aesthetic features, such as impulsive brushwork or splattered paint. For a start, despite the mythologisation of 'action painting', not all 'unconscious' imagery, even of this kind, has to be the result of an obviously automatic or spontaneous process.[11] But there could still be an important difference in psychological effect between paintings that display some kind of unconscious symbolism, for example in the somewhat iconographic way that early Surrealist works did, and paintings that present a more implicate or embodied structure. Ehrenzweig's ideas go much further in offering a psychoanalytic explanation of these effects than most other writers of his generation.

There is a further issue about the relationship between conscious and unconscious form-creation as analysed by Ehrenzweig that needs to be brought up here. Like other writers from the orthodox psychoanalytic tradition, Ehrenzweig assumes a model of psychic functioning where already existing unconscious processes are represented in consciousness, where depth content insinuates itself into surface form. The existence of repressive mechanisms, however sophisticated, is confirmation of this. But other, very different, assumptions are possible.

One is that the relation is inverse: that certain kinds of form, or aesthetic properties, suggest an antecedent 'unconscious' process of formation which is actually a creative projection (or retrojection) on our part. In other words, on the basis of certain aesthetic features, such as inarticulate form, we 'read' an unconscious history into certain paintings. This depends on understanding that expression or 'communication' in art are two-way processes: that it is not just the artist who consciously or unconsciously imbues his or her work with certain psychological contents, but that the work itself, both in process and in its final form, suggests or dictates these, both to the artist and to the spectator.

Another version of this is that there is no 'depth', that everything takes place on one continuous surface, over which there are fluctuating shifts. This is an idea that Ehrenzweig throws out in his first book but never follows up (Ehrenzweig 1967, p.173). In Chapter Seven we shall see some answers to these questions given by thinkers such as Jean-François Lyotard. But even in the next chapter, we shall see that James Hillman's strategies for working with the image pivot much more on the specific and immediate presentation of the image than on notions of some underlying 'unconscious' symbolism.

Like Hannah Segal, whose contributions he acknowledges, Ehrenzweig treats the relation between the 'beautiful' and 'ugly' components of aesthetic experience as complementary rather than mutually exclusive. For both ugliness is a powerful souvenir of conflicts to which the artwork presents a more or less successful solution, and thus contributes to the aliveness of its expression (Segal 1992). Likewise his account of the psychological repercussions of aesthetic experience goes far deeper than any account of appreciation in purely formal terms. In the next chapter we shall see how a very different perspective – that of archetypal psychology – also gives a cardinal importance to aesthetic experience and, in its more radical forms, comes up with its own version of the psychological importance of 'ugliness'.

Endnotes

1. A single and important exception is Marion Milner, who has frequently acknowledged her debt to Ehrenzweig (for example, Milner 1987)
2. A number of important testimonies to Ehrenzweig's influence on art teaching were gathered at a conference, 'Art's Hidden Order', organised by the Centre for Psychotherapeutic Studies, University of Sheffield in September 1996.
3. The Gestalt psychology of perception holds that at any given moment significant 'figures' are sought out and defined against a more inchoate background (see, for example, Arnheim 1969, pp.27–31).
4. Many of Ehrenzweig's (1977 (1953)) examples in his first book are drawn from music, and I shall not be referring to these.
5. Actually, Ehrenzweig is inconsistent on this point: he claims to be able to remember the original impressions Brahms' music made on him, despite their being subsequently smoothed out (Ehrenzweig 1967, pp.72–3).
6. See Damisch 1998 for a discussion of this contradiction.
7. This scenario is elaborated at greater length earlier in the same book (Ehrenzweig 1967, pp.64–5).
8. The various attempts to supply an alternative justification for aesthetics in a world that is no longer seen as subject to divine providence is a central theme of eighteenth and nineteenth century philososophy (Bowie 1990).
9. At one point Nietzsche actually says: 'Our estheticians have nothing to say about this grand return [to original Oneness], about the fraternal union in tragedy of the two deities, or about the alternation of Apollonian and Dionysiac excitation in the spectator' (Nietzsche 1956, p.133).
10. For a view of the differences between the two kinds of knowing, see Young 1993.
11. An interesting attempt to undo these habitual associations in relation to poetic inspiration is in James Hillman and Clayton Eshleman's dialogue in *Sulfur 16*.

Chapter Five

Aesthetics, Beauty and Soul

> For beauty is nothing
>
> but the start of dread, which we can hardly bear,
>
> and we are amazed by, because it so coolly disdains
>
> to wipe us out (Rilke, First Duino Elegy, my translation).

In the last chapter we saw how Ehrenzweig explained that inarticulate form was subject to disqualification and repression. For the archetypal psychologist James Hillman the subject of repression is beauty itself: '... the most significant unconscious today, that factor which is most important but most unrecognised in the world of our psychological culture, could be defined as 'beauty', for that is what is ignored, omitted, absent' (Hillman 1998, p.263).

Likewise, if the slackening of the barriers between depth and surface can produce effects that Ehrenzweig described as therapeutic so, as far as Hillman is concerned, the recovery of beauty, or rather of the repressed aesthetic need to experience it, is therapeutic. This is not only because it answers a fundamental need, but because beauty is a quality inherent in phenomena themselves, and ignoring or neglecting such aesthetic qualities – what he calls 'anaesthesia' – results in serious problems on both an individual and a collective scale.

Hillman rejects the whole perspective of projective psychology, according to which beauty is a subjective response, in favour of one that acknowledges its objective presence in the world: '... suppose we were to imagine that beauty is permanently given, inherent to the world in its data, there on display always. This inherent radiance lights up more translucently, more intensively within certain events, particularly those events that aim to seize it and reveal it, such as art works' (Hillman 1998, p.267). Here we find again the idea, mentioned in Chapter Two, that works of art can function as condensers of an aesthetic experience of the world.

For Hillman the apprehension of beauty (and 'apprehension' strikes an appropriate note of awe) is linked with aesthetic response in an absolutely fundamental way, that is not confined within some special preserve associated with art. As he points out, '… the activity of perception or sensation in Greek is aisthesis which means at root "taking in" and "breathing in" – a "gasp", that primary aesthetic response' (Hillman 1981, p.31). Some writers agree with Hillman in seeing aesthetic reactions as such an integral part of our perception of the world that they are almost automatic: 'To the extent that every thing, every place, every event is experienced by an aware body with sensory directness and immediate significance, it has an aesthetic element' (Berleant 1990).

It is also important to bear in mind that these aesthetic responses are not triggered only by attractive or pleasant things: they may equally be set off by ungraceful or ugly things, or even by things that are dull, bland or banal. Such aesthetic responses are not merely the psychological accompaniment to plea-surable or unpleasurable sensations, they are psychological in a more funda-mental way that fits with Bachelard's (1969b) claim that the image 'touches the depth before it stirs the surface', (p.xix) and one that connects with psyche as soul: '… psyche is the life of our aesthetic responses, that sense of taste in relation with things, that thrill or pain, disgust or expansion of breast, those primordial aesthetic reactions of the heart are soul itself speaking' (Hillman 1981, p.25).

For Hillman 'soul' is not the exclusive property of human beings and their inner worlds: it is manifest in the world outside, in the 'face' that things present to us, to which we respond. Yet even here 'soul' is not an independent entity, as it is in its theological sense, but rather a quality of experience: 'Though I cannot identify soul with anything else, I also can never grasp it by itself apart from other things, perhaps because it is like a reflection in a flowing mirror, or like the moon which mediates only borrowed light' (Hillman 1975, p.x). Though Hillman has not written specifically about it, this description of soul is strikingly similar to the connection between aesthetic response and the material qualities of works of art made by writers such as Merleau-Ponty (see Chapter Two).

As an imaginal psychologist – that is, someone whose focus is the manifesta-tions of psyche as image, and the archetypal realm of imagination they stem from – Hillman has some important things to say about the differences between the sense perception in relation to external reality and the sensory idiom of dream, phantasy and 'inner' reality. In several key articles about working with such images,[1] he writes about how the gamut of sense perception is subtly altered in dreams:

> We do not literally see images or hear metaphors; we perform an operation of insight which is a seeing-through or hearing-into. The sense-words see and hear themselves become metaphors because, at one and the same time, we are

using our senses and also not using them as we may believe we are (Hillman 1979a, p.130).

I think that there are comparable processes of 'translation' involved when we look at paintings (as mentioned in Chapter Two). This applies most obviously to representational works, where one might expect a painting to be something more complicated than a mere recreation of the artist's 'original' experience of the scene (hence the limited value of juxtaposing photographs of Mte St Victoire with Cézanne's paintings of it, or of the interior of Le Cannet with Bonnard's versions). Different kinds of translation may apply to non-representational works; this is a subject I shall return to in Chapter Eight.

Beauty, ugliness and the aesthetic response to art

Hillman's passionate call for the re-animation of the world and for the psychological, if not therapeutic, necessity for recovering aesthetic response nevertheless still carries echoes of the traditional identification of 'aesthetic' with 'beautiful'. He tries hard to extricate beauty from its identifications with works of art or specially singled-out occasions, returning us to the necessary aesthetic aspect of our perception of the world: 'Beauty is the manifest anima mundi [world's soul] – and do notice here it is neither transcendent to the manifest or hiddenly immanent within, but refers to appearances as such, created as they are, in the forms with which they are given...' (Hillman 1981, p.28). But in his arguments the old idea that there is a kind of natural congruence between beauty and truth or goodness is still taken as a working assumption.

It is, of course, important to acknowledge that beauty has formed, and still does form, an important part of the aesthetic appeal of art; and yet one of the defining features of modern art is that the criteria for 'beauty' (or 'balance', 'order' or any other comparable term) have become so open to question, so subject to contestation. Along with this, as we saw in Chapter One, its moral connotations have also been undermined. Aesthetic qualities have for a long time been as much to do with the translation or 'feel' of energies other than those which can be identified as strictly psychological (for example, political or cultural), and this has been intensified by Modernism's complex relation to industrial energies and processes. For example, the idiom of machinery, not only in Futurism, but in Leger's or even Paul Klee's work, is one obvious instance. Simple oppositions between beauty and ugliness misconstrue these qualities.

Hillman himself admits that it is ugliness that often strikes the eye most forcefully, and that it is a sign, in Plotinus' words of 'going over to another order' (Hillman 1981, p.38). Since the presented face of things and our aesthesis of them is so immediate, it is tempting to make a spontaneous identification between aesthetic and psychological discrimination: 'As important as the reflective understanding of where we are is a sensitivity to when we go over to another order. Here the relation to ugliness guides our self-knowledge. Ugliness is the guide because aesthetic responses occur most strongly in relation with the ugly' (Hillman 1981, p.39). There is an ambiguity here, as to whether ugliness is the sign of something 'wrong' (and the word has both aesthetic and moral associations) that needs to be put right, or is, rather, the sign of a distress that may be inevitable.

Hillman certainly encourages us to trust our immediate aesthetic response to the face of things in the outer world: 'Aesthetic reactions are responses to this face, and moral responsibility begins in these responses of disgust, delight, abhorrence, attraction – the spontaneous judgement of the heart' (Hillman 1981, p.40). This, to him, justifies the expansion or extraversion of 'therapy', so that it now has an obligation to look to the actual, environmental factors causing distress, rather than to read such things as symbolic of inner, psychological conflicts. It is hard to argue against his contention that much ugliness in both the man-made and natural environments are both the cause and the effect of psychological disturbance.

This could easily lead to a privileging of the beautiful over the ugly, or to the idea that ugliness must be avoided or even transformed. Hence Hillman asks, 'does not this suggest that whatever we turn from and deny becomes thereby ugly? And does not this as well suggest that what we turn toward may become beautiful?' (Hillman 1998, p.272). This notion that ugliness in the world is calling for our attention, in order that it be rescued or redeemed is a clarion call for the anima mundi to be respected; but how does it affect the roles of ugliness in art? The idea that mere 'attention' to what is ugly will lead to its transformation into something 'beautiful' feels like a sleight of hand when applied to painting. It defuses the discordant, objectionable aspect of ugliness, and glosses over the fact that in Modernist aesthetics the raw and the awkward contribute as much, or more, to a work's effects as the balanced or the lovely. As we saw in the previous chapters, both object-relations and Ehrenzweig's aesthetics offer a more convincing account of the necessary and dynamic role of ugliness in art.

I think Hillman also over-simplifies the relationship between works of art and the world at large. Ugliness, or the depiction of 'ugly' or barren scenes in paintings (for example in the industrial landscapes of L S Lowry or Prunella Clough) cannot be reduced to mere reflections of the urban wasteland: on the contrary, they try to alert us to what a superficial reaction of aversion will make us miss. At the same time, they present their own aesthetic qualities, however grey or dull they may at first appear. Just as the painting of a picturesque landscape is more than a reproduction of the original experience of nature, so the transmutational power of art has something to do with the interplay of its own intrinsic aesthetic properties, and not just with a redirection of our attention to a neglected aspect of the material world.

In addition, we once more come up against the problem that the discourse of archetypal psychology invites, if it does not actually depend on, narrative and figurative styles of imagination: for example in the kinds of animating, personifying and mythologising strategies proposed by Hillman in relation to dream and phantasy (Hillman 1983, pp.53–8). How this connects with the ways in which we might try writing about aesthetic qualities and their psychological repercussions will be dealt with in Chapter Eight. I am not, of course, suggesting that Hillman is insensitive to abstract painting (I know he is not), but rather that when he connects painting too closely with the external world, or to our fantasies about that world, there is the danger of some kind of moral agenda intruding.

However, Hillman does usually insist that there are important differences between our responses to the qualities of actual things, be they man-made or natural, and our response to images in dreams or phantasies. It is part of the project of archetypal psychology to 'see' memories, symptoms and even events as images, and not to be captured by their literal aspects, and there is no reason why this should not include aesthetic features, from the specific details of their 'face' to the style, or mythical perspective in which they might be seen. The question then is, as was the case with previous psychoanalytic ways of working with images, whether there are significant differences between dreams, phantasies and the like and works of art?

Hillman's approach is avowedly image-centered and aesthetic, and he credits psyche with an inventiveness and accuracy that consciousness or intellectual analysis often interferes with, thus rendering it 'unconscious' (Hillman 1983, p.53). Thus, there is less discrepancy between the working of psyche in dream and its working in art in his account than in the perspective of traditional psychoanalysis. Indeed archetypal psychology attaches more importance to the idea that images from the world of art may be more appropriate and informative avenues to psyche than clinical material, with all its local deformations and diversions (see for example Cobb 1992).

The aesthetics of pathology and pathologising

One of Hillman's most provocative conceptual reversals in this respect is his notion of 'pathologising'. Here pathology, with all its signs of sickness, deformity and aberration, symptoms that the patient passively suffers, is translated, in the imaginal dimension of soul, into an active display of images. Hillman defines pathologising as '… the psyche's autonomous ability to create illness, morbidity, disorder, abnormality and suffering in any aspect of its behaviour and to experience and imagine life through this deformed and afflicted perspective' (Hillman 1975, p.57).

The important thing here is that such images are not literal, and that just as our response to images in dreams or fantasies should not be governed by the laws of external perception, so our reaction to these pathologised images should not be to correct them or put them right, but to explore their particular natures imaginatively.

Hillman himself has not explored how pathologising might be manifested in art, and especially painting, but several of his colleagues have (for example Cobb 1992; Lopez-Pedraza 1996; Maclagan 1989b). The crucial point is that, even in dreams and fantasies, the psyche uses complaints to speak in a magnified and misshapen language about its depths (Hillman 1975, p.82). Hence pathologising has a rhetorical or even melodramatic cast to it. This is something that art would tend to highlight, in both its aesthetic and its psychological manifestations.

One of the advantages of this concept of pathologising is that it avoids the kind of identifications between an artist's work and his or her life or person that start off so many psychological interpretations of art on the wrong track. Art has, over the last couple of centuries, begun to concentrate on forms of suffering that are 'personal' and 'psychological' rather than being attributed to divine retribution or tragic catastrophe. Conflicts which were previously seen in terms of a relation between the individual and some collective or transcendent force (God, fate or the spectre of history) have become interiorised and thus give the impression that they are purely personal. While pathologising must, presumably, manifest itself on a collective level, it has come to be seen in increasingly particular terms.

This has probably contributed to the distorted image of the tormented artist and to the subjectifying of much pathologising imagery in painting (Goya, Gericault, Ensor and Redon are some of the more obvious early instances). This tendency has been exacerbated by the frequently anti-social or adversarial stance of Modernism (of which Surrealism is an obvious early example, and Outsider Art perhaps the final manifestation).

The 'pathological' elements of an artist's work, even, or above all, where they are flagrant (in the paintings of Schiele, Bacon or Clemente, to give some more recent examples) cannot be simply tracked back to personal forms of suffering or disorder without losing just that metaphoric and imaginal resonance that results from their being works of art rather than symptoms or dreams.[2] This is a fundamental feature, prior to any theatrical sense of the artist as putting on the agony.

In addition to these archetypal aspects of today's psyche, there are also well documented historical and cultural influences: the widespread dissemination, in the early twentieth century, of psychoanalytic ideas and even of case studies, along with a burgeoning literature on clinical psychopathology (such as Kraepelin, Krafft-Ebbing and Havelock Ellis). Modernist artists, whose lifestyle and work had already been tarred with this brush, often 'adopted' pathologised imagery in ways that were bound to have a histrionic or ironic aspect to them.[3] Psychotic art, in its classic instances (Wölfli, Aloise, Ramirez), where patients/artists are supposed to be in the grip of instinctual form-creating mechanisms, or driven by compulsions over which they have no control, might seem to be an obvious exception to this. But psychotic art (and indeed psychotic hallucinations) are not exempt from cultural influences which may, in some cases (such as Wölfli) have a kind of rhetorical aspect to them (see Maclagan 1997).

Once again, we must remember that works of art are translations: beyond both the immediacy of external world perception and the rehearsals of this experience that are supposedly decanted into phantasy and dreaming. They are thus pre-eminently suited to be both sources of pathologising and vehicles for it: 'The crazy artist, the daft poet and mad professor are neither romantic clichés nor antibourgeois postures. They are metaphors for the intimate relation between pathologising and imagination. Pathologising processes are a source of imaginative work, and the work provides a container for the pathologising processes' (Hillman 1975, p.107). Pathologising in art does not simply have to do with imagery as such – with an iconography of figures that are grotesque or perverse, or with claustrophobic interiors or lurid landscapes – it is also present at a stylistic level. In other words, it has its own characteristic aesthetic spectrum.

All of this raises serious doubts about the labelling of certain stylistic features of art as 'psychopathological'. The point at issue here is really one about the danger of translating formal features, such as compacting, repetition or distortion, straight into quasi-clinical judgements. Even in Prinzhorn's day, once 'psychotic art' was disconnected from its clinical context, it proved almost impossible to distinguish it from the work of avant-garde artists (see Chapter One). I would take this as far as to say that the label 'psychotic', as applied to a painting or drawing per se is now more of a descriptive or stylistic label than a psychiatric diagnosis.

It also raises some questions about 'madness' in relation to art. The classic image of the psychotic artist, based as it was on such exceptional figures as

Adolf Wölfli or Aloise Corbaz, is something like a compressed and distorted version of the heroic image of the post-Renaissance creative artist: someone driven to create, compulsively productive, living an idiosyncratic existence (see Maclagan 1997, pp.131–144). The traditional convergence between genius and madness reaches a sort of apogee in the figure of psychotic creators and their work, isolated and driven in upon themselves by confinement.

But this 'madness' is something much wider and more diverse than the psychiatric categorisations of it allow;[4] nor is it necessarily something psychopathological. As we saw in Chapter Two, some forms of aesthetic experience have a rapturous, ecstatic feel to them that could, in other contexts, be called 'mad'. So too does the experience of making art: normal boundaries between subject and object are suspended in the 'manic-oceanic' phase of the creative process. There may even be, as Ehrenzweig pointed out, something therapeutic about this.

An aesthetics of pathologising seems to offer many mansions for such madness to inhabit. Take, for instance, the traditional notion of melancholy and its modern version, depression. Surely we can see Max Beckmann's work, for example, as an extended meditation on such Saturnine themes, and feel how they are embodied, not only in the imagery of many of his paintings, with their uncanny mix of world-weary sensuality, shop-soiled mythology and occult references, but also in their facture and aesthetic qualities. Not only do many of his paintings use a sombre, almost sullied palette of colour, and heavily accentuated black outlines, but his working technique sometimes involves passages of paintwork that are repeatedly scraped and repainted.

Because pictorial psychopathology was originally defined in relation to norms of representation and figurative symbolism, pathologising seems particularly suited to artworks that work with such terms, especially when they twist or deform them. If this is the area in which Hillman's concept seems most at home, to what extent can it be applied to non-figurative art? Calling abstract forms 'twisted' or 'distorted', or calling colours 'sombre', 'livid' or 'sickly', while apparently an appropriate vocabulary for pathologising, can be open to contention.

Furthermore, the relatively unconventional nature of some abstract painting leaves its psychological resonances floating and open to the incursion of personal meanings justified by biographical context. A good example is the way in which exactly this floating, elusive quality in Arshile Gorky's late paintings, with their suggestive titles, has been tethered to the tragic circumstances of his life (Coles 1990). Another is Rothko's famous late abstract paintings, where the dissolution of form and the shadowy key of colour is often read in the light (or darkness) of his suicide.

However, because Hillman's strategy, at least in relation to dreams, is to use imagery to deal with an image, rather than translating it into concepts, the way is open to use phantasy as a way of exploring a painting. In particular, Hillman insists that we attend to the specifics of an image, and in this context this means not just its imaginal detail (this kind of snake, moving this way), but to its specific aesthetics. This avoids the risk of it being read only in terms of an archetypal iconography. As we shall see in Chapter Eight, fantasies about a work of art are not just ways of elaborating its psychological resonances: they are also ways of getting a handle on its aesthetic qualities (Maclagan 1989).

Pathologising stands in a provocative position in relation to psychiatric and even psychoanalytic concepts about psychic disturbance and disorder. It dislocates normative assumptions about the connection between the 'pathology' of images and the sickness of the person who made them. It also offers us ways of ensuring that the connections between aesthetic and psychological qualities remain flexible and yet faithful. In the next chapter we shall be looking at some of the ways in which a practice of art that is to some extent artificially induced – art therapy – connects the aesthetic and psychological aspects of the pictorial image.

Endnotes

1. The articles in question are: 'An inquiry into image' (1977), 'Further notes on images' (1978) and 'Image sense' (1979a). They form part of a work in progress, the publication of which has long been promised.
2. Of course, such 'not-me' aspects of dreams or symptoms can be seen as part of their salutary effect: this is certainly a key element in archetypal therapy.
3. For a brief, but incisive treatment of these issues in relation to Schiele's work see Schroder 1999.
4. The obvious reference here is to Michel Foucault's (1972) work, but see also Sass 1992.

Chapter Six

Art Therapy and the Therapy of Art

The psychological mechanisms from which artistic creation proceeds are, it seems to me, such that we should either classify them once and for all in the domain of the pathological, and consider the artist in every case as a psychopath, or else widen our conception of what is healthy and normal, and push its limit so far back that the whole of madness can find a place therein. (Dubuffet 1951)

Most of what I have written so far about the psychological aspects of aesthetics deals with works of art that have not been specifically addressed to any therapeutic situation. Such a situation is one in which works of art are viewed from a particular psychological perspective which is narrower, deeper and more specialised than what I have so far included under the heading of 'psychological'. In classical psychoanalysis this involved the enlisting of already created works as evidence for its new theories about unconscious processes. In most cases this evidence was historical, and the artist in question was dead, so that the application of psychotherapeutic concepts to their work was a largely theoretical enterprise. In art therapy, artworks are created specifically for a therapeutic context in which these processes are of more actual importance. In Freud's writings about art its psychoaesthetic qualities are invoked as a support for psychoanalytic theory; in art therapy these qualities are attended to in order to understand and help the patient. Nevertheless, it could be argued that in both instances there are factors that give a special focus and perspective to the understanding of art. Some of these are internal, in that they are part of the professional slant of psychotherapy: for example, models of the dynamics of unconscious processes and of the nature of the therapeutic relationship. Others are external, for example, to do with expectations of healing or the demands of mental health service provision.

Psychoanalysis and art: from theory to practice

Art's interest for psychoanalysis was essentially an internal, 'applied' one, in which works of art served as a cultural backdrop to its theories of unconscious processes. They also served to construct a kind of pedigree, whereby such processes could be shown to pre-date Freud, and in the case of the famous Oedipus complex, to extend as far back as antiquity.[1] While Freud frequently paid tribute to the psychological insights of previous poets and artists, he gave the impression that he was confident that his theories provided a more systematic and 'scientific' picture of unconscious thinking than they had done.

More than that, it could be said that the ingenuity of Freud's methods for interpreting of artworks – a suitable match for the ways in which 'unconscious' meaning is, by definition, un-reasonable – amounted to an alternative creative 'work'. This is reinforced by the fact, noted in Chapter Three, that Freudian theories about the translation of unconscious material into consciousness in the dream-work owe a great deal to the symbolic devices of traditional fine art. It is also significant that, although Freud recommended that psychoanalytic studies should take second-rate works as their subject, where there were plenty of chinks in the artist's armour, his own texts deal almost exclusively with such masters as Leonardo, Michelangelo and Dostoievsky. Although such studies – and Freud's were not the first – look at first like combinations of art-historical and clinical perspectives, there are in fact some important differences between the two.

The psychoanalytic use of works of art as 'case studies' is suspect for several reasons. First of all, the posthumous study of an artist, based on what are often fragmentary biographical details, is deprived of the actual therapeutic relation-ship and the spontaneous associations on which analysis proper hinges, and has to depend on speculative (re)constructions of infantile deprivation, trauma or phantasy which are largely deduced from their work. Here psychoanalysis is open to the charge of discovering what it has already 'planted', in the sense that its hermeneutic method starts off with an already given stock of unconscious motifs, and then proceeds to find them in the work of art, by hook or by crook. Second, Freud was convinced that pictorial images were, as a means of commu-nication, inferior to language. The reason the pictorial idiom of dreams was so confusing was that '… all the verbal apparatus by means of which the more subtle thought-relations are expressed; the conjunctions and prepositions, the variations of declension and conjugation, are lacking, because the means of representing them is absent…' (Freud).

However a work of art is not usually trying to 'communicate' in such a straightforward fashion: despite the tradition of 'ut pictura poeisis' (every picture should tell a story), it does not necessarily aspire to being like a language. Indeed there is a whole contrary tradition of pictorial symbolism (for example, that of Renaissance neo-Platonism[2]) which holds that the comprehensive and multivalent character of images is precisely their strong point. Once again, Freud here displays what I have called his 'iconographic prejudice' (Chapter Three).

Third, a work of art is not as unwitting a construction as is a dream: the artist is better equipped than the dreamer, and not simply because he or she is conscious. Freud was forced to allow that artists might have an unusual 'flexibility of repression' that allowed more material that was more coloured by the unconscious to emerge. In addition, of course, they possess special skills and experience that help them reshape this material. While Freud's initial treatment of this expertise (which obviously includes the manipulation of aesthetic qualities) was somewhat dismissive, in his later writing about art and literature he accorded greater respect to the artist's mysterious powers – perhaps because they were something he felt himself to share in.

Art and therapy in Jungian practice

The interest of psychoanalysis in art is thus a mixture of the cultural and the clinical, and in a sense a virtual one: nor do paintings or drawings play any central role in actual psychoanalytic therapy.[3] However, things are very different when we come to Jung, for whom the image was both a fundamental aspect of psyche, and the natural idiom of 'non-directed' or phantasy thinking. On the basis of his own experience of channelling irruptions of unconscious material through writing and painting them out,[4] Jung began recommending to some of his patients that they do the same. Not all patients were suited for this, but those for whom the path of the 'creative formulation' of phantasy material beckoned could use painting, drawing and modelling as ways of making bridges between their conscious and unconscious minds.

Most of Jung's patients, in contrast with the psychotics he had got to know at the Burgholzli hospital, came from cultivated backgrounds where a certain 'amateur' familiarity with the practice of painting and music could be expected (Lanteri-Laura 1984, pp.13–14). Painting was a way of furthering the image, of encouraging the original unconscious material to be '... continually varied and increased until a kind of condensation of motifs into more or less stereotyped symbols takes place' (Jung 1960, pp.84). The important thing was that the image should be worked on as well as possible, even if this took some time. However, it should not on that account be regarded as art. As we saw in Chapter One, Jung made determined efforts to insulate the aesthetic from the psychological aspects of such work.

Jung's suspicion of the artistic was not just aimed at an irresponsible 'aesthetic attitude' towards the finished work; it was also based on his experience that unconscious material tended, on its emergence into consciousness, to be overvalued, particularly when it took on visual form. It is true that patients can sometimes be fascinated by the impact of images they have made, and part of this may be due to their aesthetic qualities.

This can happen in a particularly dramatic way with people in a psychotic state, where powerful imagery is so disconnected from the person themselves that it seems to be dictated. Clearly, a good deal depends upon the relationship a person has to their artwork: neither so close as to be completely identified with it, nor so dissociated that it appears utterly other. Negotiating this space between artist and artwork is something that a therapeutic setting can assist in a variety of ways.

Jung nevertheless believed that intellectual interpretation and creative formulation were counterparts in a 'compensatory relationship' (Jung 1960, p.85). In Chapter Eight we shall see how this is worked out in the mutual modification of aesthetic features and the phantasies that play about them. The fact that he concedes that 'often the hands know how to solve a riddle with which the intellect has wrestled in vain' (p.86), also goes some way towards mitigating the antagonism in his writings between the aesthetic and the psychological, in the sense that I am using the terms.

If patients can be seduced by the aesthetic impact of pictures that emerge when unconscious material surfaces into consciousness, so can therapists, and sometimes their concern for the patient may be eclipsed by fascination with the imagery they produce. This is illustrated by the case of Joseph Henderson, the Jungian analyst who treated Jackson Pollock for alchoholism in 1939–40, and who later admitted that he was so impressed by his patient's striking archetypal imagery that he might have neglected to tackle his underlying psychological problems, for fear of stopping their flow.[5]

There is a question here, not only about how far any patient's imagery is to be treated as their personal expression, as opposed to a more generic or archetypal one, but also about to whom these images ultimately belong. What may have been created in a context where art was a means to another end sometimes turns out also to be valuable in and for itself. This is presumably one of the reasons that justifies the exhibition of psychotic art or patient art.

In a therapeutic context, this also raises the problem that we encountered in Chapter One, where I argued that an artist's work cannot be understood simply as an expression of his or her individual history. This is true even of the twists and turns of symptomatology. As James Hillman (1975) reminds us

... the symptoms and quirks are both me and not me – both most intimate and shameful and a revelation of my deeps, steering my fate through character so that I cannot shrug them off. Yet they are not of my intention: they are visitations, alienations, bringing home the personal/impersonal paradox of the soul... (p.105)

If this is true of symptoms, then it is even more true for artworks. From an archetypal perspective, the interest of a painting is not as a form of self-expression, but as something almost opposite: as a testimony to a dimension of psyche beyond the individual.

Indeed, he has gone so far as to assert that 'These images make one realize that the patient, me, you, is only relatively real. The images are what really really count, and they get so little place in our world, so my job is to let them speak and to speak with them' (Hillman 1983, p.52). Hillman is talking about all sorts of images in therapy – memories, dreams fantasies – not just the tangible ones that art therapy is involved with; however, the distinction is in some ways irrelevant because all such images can have an inherent fascination. But because artworks have a material, independent existence, their aesthetic properties may have an even more objective status.

This can lead to some difficult ethical problems when works made in therapeutic or psychiatric settings (such as Leo Navratil's Artist's House at Gugging[6]) are exhibited for their artistic qualities, while at the same time their clinical provenance is also an important factor in their interest (Maclagan 1995). It can sometimes look as if the appetite for Outsider Art, for example, is driven by purely 'aesthetic' concerns; as though it is valued only for its formal originality and extremity, regardless of the psychological cost to the artist concerned.

But I think that its psychological impact is also a factor; and here our relation to certain forms of patient art is no more and no less 'cruel' than our relation to the individual suffering behind many other kinds of art. But because of the intensity of patient distress or disturbance, there is strong pressure to identify therapeutic art with the expression of individual suffering. It sometimes looks as if our concern for the confidentiality of patient art is a mirror-image of the almost aggressive curiosity we have about the personal details of artist's lives.

Art and the pioneer phase of art therapy

What made Jung a reference point for the later development of 'art therapy' was not just his insistence on the primacy of the image and the phantasy thinking that depends on it, nor the enormous importance he attached to archetypal symbolism, but his pioneering promotion of art making as an important path to psychological awareness. However, because of the psyche's tendency to self-regulation, an individual could embark on this path outside any therapeutic relationship.

Even within a therapeutic setting, there are significant differences between Jung's practice and the current clinical application of art therapy. One is that art therapy is usually much less directive (Jung sometimes told his patients to make a picture on a certain theme); another is that the cultural background and artistic disposition of today's patients are very different; a third is that the art is now almost always made in the therapy session (Jung's patients would bring in pictures made beforehand). Modern art therapy also tends to relate the artwork much more closely to the vicissitudes of the therapeutic relationship, whereas for Jung transference was less central to its understanding.

Art therapy as such has its origins in the post-war period, with the work of artists such as Adrian Hill, Edward Adamson, E M Lydiatt, Rita Simon, Michael Edwards and John Henzell, who began working in psychiatric hospitals, convalescent wards and educational settings.[7] While all of these pioneers learned about psychiatric and psychoanalytic (and even in Henzell's case, anti-psychiatric) theories, it was their experience and expertise as artists who understood image-making from the inside that mattered most.

Indeed it is fair to say that in this early phase it was the experience of creating, the handling of the medium and the process of the work's materialisation that were credited with most of art's therapeutic effects. The art therapist's contribution was discreet and subliminal: what mattered was the creation and maintenance of an encouraging and therapeutic environment, made tangible in the character of the art room itself, in which patients could work at their own pace with a minimum of comment or regulation. Today, with the closure of so many large psychiatric hospitals, such studio spaces are rare.[8]

Such art studios were, in effect, asylums within the asylum, and in many instances the work remained exempt from any professional assessment, either psychiatric or artistic. An extreme instance was the situation of Adamson at the Netherne, where as part of an experiment in the psychiatric diagnosis of artwork, he was instructed not to talk to patients about their work (Waller 1991, pp.54–5). Partly because of the withdrawn and institutionalised character of many of the patients (it was almost as if 'art therapy reaches the patients other therapies cannot reach'), there was a respect among art therapists for those fragile, tacit aspects of art's significance that could not easily be put into words. This goes some way towards explaining why so little was written at the time about the practice of early art therapy. There was, in any case, no real forum for such writing, since the first issue of *Inscape* (the journal of the British Association of Art Therapists) was only published in 1969.

Although art therapy work was produced under the aegis of 'art', it was effectively insulated from the outside world of art, or at least connected with it only peripherally and incidentally, for example by occasional exhibitions.[9] Nevertheless, the easy-going, open-ended atmosphere of many traditional art therapy studios, and the unscheduled time that many patients were able to spend there reproduced many of the conditions under which more professional art is created: a protected space, freedom from scrutiny, the opportunity to experiment and the absence of any obvious therapeutic agenda.

While many of the patients might have come with an initial suspicion or fear of 'art' that derived from their previous educational and cultural disqualification, the flexible pace and permissive background of the art room did much to enable work of real aesthetic quality to be created. Thus art therapy, in its early, free-range state, did tap into a subliminal reservoir of creativity that was independent of any professional training or cultural support. It is all the more unjust, then, for partisans of Outsider Art such as Jean Dubuffet, Victor Musgrave or Michel Thévoz to claim that art therapy stifles or normalises creativity.

This early situation of voluntary exile from the world of art did enable the connections between aesthetic and psychological factors to be explored in a much more open-minded way than would have been possible under the official aegis of either psychotherapy or art. Such explorations tended to be ad hoc, tentative and particular, avoiding any kind of reading that might smack of the literalism of psychiatric diagnoses or the obstinacy of psychoanalytic interpretations. Retrospective accounts such as Lyddiatt (1971) or Simon (1992) convey something of this. The challenge of finding ways of conveying this often intuitive sense-making in words without nailing it down in programmatic concepts is one that will be addressed in Chapter Eight.

The professionalisation of art therapy

With the development of art therapy into a profession one might expect this kind of attention to the psychological reverberations of art's aesthetic features to play an important part in its training and in the burgeoning art therapy literature. Yet this turns out to be far from the case. Art therapy today has forged increasingly close links with psychotherapy, with its developmental scenarios and its emphasis on the therapeutic relationship. To some extent this is prompted by external factors, such as the need for art therapy to establish its credentials alongside other helping professions. But there is also, I think, a dynamic internal to art therapy: a need to justify itself in more objective terms.

This gives a special slant to both the aesthetic and the psychological understanding of art; one that is all too often led by the clinical situation. When psychotherapeutic concepts are used, for example in the case of object-relations theory, which is the perspective most often adopted in art therapy literature, it is seldom to explore the formal dynamics of the artwork itself in any depth. There is a parallel here with early 'applied' psychoanalysis, where the work of art was subordinated to a clinical agenda. More and more it feels as if the 'art' in art therapy is being at best taken for granted, or at worst overlooked. In the published literature there is only a handful of writers (Allen 1995; Henzell 1994; McNiff 1992; Simon 1992, for example) who concentrate on the central psychological significance of aesthetic qualities.

Mention should be made here of Arthur Robbins's concept of 'psychoaesthetics' (Robbins 1994). His concept of the intimate relation between aesthetic features of artworks and psychological states, whether of health or of pathology, is similar to the one I put forward in this book: indeed I occasionally use the term myself. However, he uses it to refer at one and the same time to the aesthetic features of a patient's artwork and to the qualities of the therapeutic relationship at any given moment.

There is, of course a connection between the two, and it is certainly important to be able to focus on the 'aesthetic structure' of a therapeutic communication rather than just its content (Robbins 1994, p.61). But there are too many other kinds of information – body language, tone of voice, counter-transference imagery – to enable us to catch more than glimpses of Robbins responding to the aesthetics of an artwork in itself, independent of its context. For him the two are clearly not to be separated.

To take another example, this time from the field of archetypal psychology, which might be presumed to be more sympathetic to these qualities: Mary Watkins (1981) sketches half-a-dozen possible fates of the pictorial image in a therapeutic context. Here she rightly contrasts an imaginal approach with more functional or goal-oriented ones:

> ... the art therapist is far from an appendage to diagnostic procedures, an arts and crafts clean-up lady, a sanitiser and straightener of images, a watchdog for impending fragmentation, or a kind, friendly presence while one paints or draws. She is someone alert not just to the literal image, but to gestures, tones of voice, ways of interacting, presenting complaints and history (p.117).

These are important clues, not usually available to the spectator of a work of art. However, all that she has to say about working with the material aesthetics of the image is that 'The art therapist should attend to the structure of an image, so that its myriad details are not seen as random expressions, distortions, or disguises, but as necessary to the precise meaning of the whole image' (p.117). In the context of an imaginal therapy this is particularly disappointing and summary.

Art, aesthetics and art therapy

The point here is not to deny the validity of 'art psychotherapy' (as art therapy is now professionally styled), or to rule out various kinds of alliance between psychotherapy or psychoanalysis and art: in purely therapeutic terms these can undoubtedly be effective. But if we are going to talk about 'art therapy', then we need to prevent the potential knowledge of the psyche intrinsic to 'art' from being eclipsed by, for example, a psychodynamic perspective. Pat Allen recently published a provocative paper, in which she claimed there was a creeping 'clinification' of art therapy. That is, where other 'clinical' skills predominate over the art, which is then relegated to an accessory status, and one that has to be justified in terms other than its own. In contrast, she claims that 'Understanding of the therapeutic potential of art media can best be gained by doing art, in a sustained, mindful and self-invested way' (Allen 1992, p.23).

Following on from this, Allen suggests that art therapists should transfer some of their own art practice to the therapeutic work space. This is rather a literal way of getting the 'art' back into art therapy, but it raises a fundamental issue: how much of the 'art' perspective is now acknowledged as crucial to art therapy? This would include, not only its attention to visible (aesthetic) qualities, but also the particular forms of psychological life that they evoke.

It is true that a background in fine art is still considered to be a prerequisite for applicants to train as art therapists, but the original context that made this relevant – the brevity of art therapy training courses – now no longer applies. On the basis of my own experience in training workshops, I am not sure that a fine art background could ever be relied on to equip students with a psychoaesthetic sensitivity to images. Furthermore, many of the current models of fine art – such as conceptual art, installation and performance art, digitally produced imagery and other post-Modernist idioms – are more distant than traditional painting was from what is likely to be encountered in art therapy settings.

Many students find that their experience as artists is effectively marginalised: most courses have little room for artistic studio practice, or space in their curricula for fostering those links with mythological and cultural symbols in art that are so vital to the archetypal psychology inspired by Jung which is supposed to be an inspiration for art therapy. In addition, the jobs they are being prepared for have changed: the institutional circumstances that once permitted long-term, open-ended art therapy work with patients have, in many cases, been replaced with external pressures for short-term, outcome-oriented work.

The sidelining of art is not confined to professional training or practice: it is also evident in the individual art therapist's relationships with art. Recent research (Gilroy 1989) suggests that many art therapists more or less abandon working as artists, or work in a much more sporadic or occasional fashion. While it would be dogmatic to claim that this has a negative effect on their practice, it certainly suggests that art has in some sense become a luxury they can no longer afford.

This is not simply due to external pressures, such as shortage of time and space, or the length of time required to complete work within any particular artist's studio practice, factors which are often real enough. It is also connected with what I would call an 'interference' between an artistic and a therapeutic relationship with the image. Part of one's mind may be too readily alerted to spot 'unconscious' imagery to be able to allow another part to create unself-consciously. It is not simply that therapy might 'disrupt the creative process' (the theme of a conference at Goldsmith's College, London recorded in *Inscape*, April 1983), but that the drying up of personal creative experience might subtly alter an art therapist's perspective (as if a psychoanalyst no longer remembered his or her own dreams).

I know from personal experience that art therapists who are also artists have, when it comes to creating their own work, to be able to 'run with the hare and hunt with the hounds'. This does not necessarily mean relying on improvisation and spontaneous execution: contrary to the popular stereotype, most creative people are able to switch back and forth between different levels of consciousness, as Ehrenzweig showed. It usually does mean that any conscious translation between aesthetic and psychological features is implicit or suspended. For example, the ways in which I personally may animate or personify forms in my work is more like a temporary scaffolding that enables certain structural decisions to be taken ('that looks too much like a monster face') than any longer-term interpretation. Perhaps such evasion is necessary in order to create with a sufficient degree of un-knowingness.

This also raises the question of whether art's therapeutic effects are confined to art therapy, or might not also be experienced in the more solitary setting of the studio. 'Therapeutic' here means something more than, for example, the cathartic discharge of emotion, self-expression or the conscious elaboration of phantasy: it must entail some significant shift in the artist's psyche, even if this is not reflected in immediate conscious insight. I would argue that the regular experience of making art, where communication of various kinds between conscious and unconscious takes place, can in itself be therapeutic in this sense.[10]

Another more dramatic way of putting this would be to say that most artists have a working relationship with madness, if by 'madness' is meant a range of experiences — the dissolution of subject–object boundaries, the magical animation of material, the manic capacity to ride the flow of inarticulate form, for example — that in other contexts would be reckoned psychotic (Maclagan 1999). Simply being able to sustain and accumulate such experiences might be as important as nourishing one's psyche by recording and working on one's own dreams. A stronger version of this contention is to be found, as we saw in Chapter Four, in Anton Ehrenzweig's belief that the artist's relationship to his artwork reproduces many of the features of an analytic relationship and thus constitutes a form of self-therapy.

Of course not many patients who come to art therapy are in any position, materially or psychologically, to go through such processes on their own: it is, as we have seen, one of the art therapist's functions to enable this. This is something more fundamental than the technical facilitation of art making, for this in turn depends on a capacity to imagine, and to trust the products of imagination, that may have been both culturally stunted and psychologically blocked. Reviving these capacities could be described as a form of aesthetic education, in that it is hoped that it will help patients become more aware of the links between the aesthetic and the psychological 'feel' of their own images, and perhaps even those of others.[11]

Yet art therapists are in a curious position: in order to try to understand the patient's artwork it is not enough simply to respond to the final product, as Jung did: they are also able to observe the process of its making. In this they exercise a privilege that is almost unique, except perhaps in certain early stages of art education, in that they can both witness the creative process at first hand and elicit reports of it immediately afterwards. This is often quite an uncomfortable moment, when the patient/artist has to shift from being more or less absorbed in his or her work to stepping away from it. It is, of course, true that for some patients this initial privacy is only possible thanks to the therapeutic situation (Winnicott's (1965) thoughts about the capacity to be alone depending on the environmental presence of another would apply here). Nevertheless, this liminal, half-private, half-public situation is quite different from that of most artists in their studios, where their relationship is exclusively with their artwork, and any audience is present only by implication.

One of the consequences of this is that it is hard for the art therapist's attention not to focus on the outward manifestations of the artistic process. Of course, knowing a picture's history is revealing: there are not only the visible (or audible) variations in a patient's pace and energy, but also possibilties of glimpsing passages that may be subsequently obliterated. But for just this reason there is a danger that the inner, imaginative recreation of the work will be correspondingly neglected. Popular fascination with films of modern artists at work demonstrates how this almost voyeuristic privileging of the outside-in perspective can distort our understanding of its aesthetic features.[12] For example, a common question in art therapy groups is 'What did you do first?', as though such first moves were primary in a more fundamental sense.

Perhaps it would be fairer to say that there are two rather different moments in making sense of a picture in art therapy. One occurs during the session itself, and may focus on the creative process, the final result and on what Joy Schaverien (1992) calls the 'disposal' of the image (pp.114–16). The other occurs some time after, for example in supervision or in writing a case study, and may have the time and space available to focus more on the picture's inherent aesthetic features. The fact that this second moment is outside the framework of the therapy session gives a kind of permission for more speculative or creative responses with which to elaborate these.

Working with aesthetic and psychological qualities in art therapy

Having expressed these reservations, I want to confirm some of the ways in which aesthetic and psychological aspects of art therapy pictures do in fact interact. First of all, aesthetic qualities are an irreplaceable clue to the 'feel' of a picture. This feeling may have powerful positive or negative impact, or it may just be banal, flat or dead. As we saw in Chapter One, it may be emotionally loaded, but it is certainly not exclusively to do with 'feelings' in this sense. It may have resonances with bodily sensations or phantasies: the artwork of some patients with eating disorders can give vivid glimpses of this (Levens 1995; Maclagan 1998a).

Often the only warrant for ascribing this 'feel' are the aesthetic properties of the picture itself. Sometimes a picture's feel agrees with what its creator intended, or is accepted by him or her after the event, or else it may be at variance, and this discrepancy can sometimes be seen as a contradiction ('unconscious' messages versus conscious ones). But at other times the aesthetic feel of a picture is much more ambiguous and hard to put into words; this is often because the feelings in question refer to a pre-verbal, or even pre-symbolic, level. The only way of handling this is through a scatter of 'readings', none of which is in itself conclusive, but which may cumulatively add up.

All of this is familiar from the way works of art in general are responded to. Art therapy is certainly not alone in experiencing the difficulties of putting aesthetic feel into words. What differences, then, does a therapeutic context make? I think that it inevitably tends to narrow the aperture of the psychological towards a focus on what will fit most readily with psychotherapeutic concepts. Perhaps this special focus is tacitly present even in open-ended situations; it is surely more salient in therapeutic settings that have one kind of agenda or another. This is, I think, what Martina Thomson (1989) meant when she wrote 'I wonder whether it is because the paintings in art therapy are always executed in a communicating relationship with the therapist that they seem to lack a certain core and are distinguishable as "therapeutic art"' (p.36).

This 'professional deformation', to borrow Cocteau's term for the poet's inclination, affects both patient and therapist: the patient may perform, sometimes quite unconsciously, to whatever expectations he or she may have of art therapy; and the therapist, sometimes equally unconsciously, may conform to what they feel is a 'proper' therapeutic perspective.

I had to struggle with these issues in my own practice. My work with one patient in particular, who has since been recognised as an Outsider artist, brought them to a head. When I first encountered him (in a therapeutic community), he spent most of the night 'doodling' intense biro or felt-tip pictures, many of which he destroyed. I recognised early on that his artwork had remarkable aesthetic quality, and that it was simply not possible to detach this from the more 'psychological' features that therapy might want to concentrate upon.

In addition, part of my efforts to help him live better with his depression involved encouraging him to value his work, and to recognise that he was not alone in his seemingly eccentric creation. When, towards the end of his work with me, he saw me at home, he sometimes asked to look into my studio (which was on the ground floor), and I would let him see some of my work and occasionally introduce him to new materials or techniques.[13] Among other things, I once or twice arranged to visit art exhibitions with him (he was particularly encouraged by the example of Paul Klee, whose work even had certain technical similarities to his own). In all these ways the worlds of art and of art therapy overlapped.

Art therapy and the wider world of art

Some interesting links have recently been forged between art therapy and the wider world of art. Rita Simon (1992), in particular, has written about fundamental 'stylistic' shifts, which may occur even within the same session, and which carry an implicit psychological significance. Her model for these 'styles' clearly derives from the ways in which they can be seen in the history of art on a wide scale (perhaps that of Malraux's 'imaginary museum'). However, they are not styles in an art-historical sense, but in a more 'aesthetic' sense. As we saw in Chapter Three, terms like 'baroque' or even 'psychotic' are descriptive or stylistic labels that apply outside and beyond the context in which they were originally used.

Simon makes an initial distinction between 'Archaic', in the sense of pictures 'with bold colours and large, simple shapes' which seem to belong to a pre-Renaissance tradition, and 'Traditional', which display a more conventional pictorial logic (such as perspective) or more careful handling. These basic stylistic contrasts are further complicated by an inclination towards either of two other modes: 'Linear', 'those dominated by lines or outlines of flat masses' or 'Massive', 'those that used colours and tones that suggested solid shapes' (Simon 1992, p.5). In practice, a picture may combine features within a general Linear or Massive style, and these might consitute 'transitional' areas; however the opposition between Archaic and Traditional remains fundamental (see Fig 6.1).

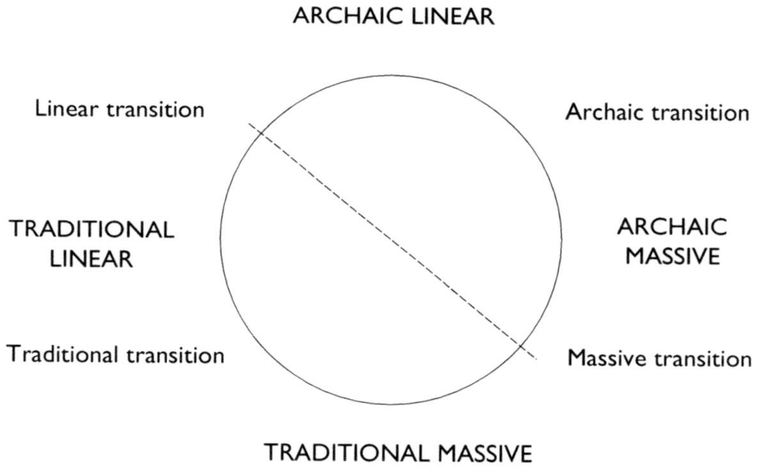

ARCHAIC LINEAR

Linear transition   Archaic transition

TRADITIONAL   ARCHAIC
LINEAR   MASSIVE

Traditional transition   Massive transition

TRADITIONAL MASSIVE

Figure 6.1 The circle of styles by Rita Simon. Reproduced with permission.

Simon's 'circle of styles' represents at the same time a cycle of psychological states. Significantly, in view of the small number of references to Jung in art therapy literature, this draws substantially on Jung's model of the four basic psychological functions (intellectual, emotional, sensuous and intuitive). To use a simple example, a picture in a strong Archaic Massive style usually expresses powerful emotion (Simon 1992, p.8). Whereas Jung's model is essentially typological, Simon's has more to do with a patient's habitual and familar ways of looking at the world, and with their capacity to shift out of them if they have somehow become stuck in them (Simon 1992, pp. 194–6). Her attention to style rather than to the figurative or symbolic vocabulary of a picture, or rather her ability to work on the interaction between them, is an important contribution to art therapy.

Simon's work offers a coherent way of making sense of the links between aesthetic and psychological features, both within and beyond a therapeutic context. I think her ideas are perfectly compatible with the more 'facture'-oriented approach of someone like Ehrenzweig: it is as if they operate on a slightly larger scale, and are more comprehensive, in that they are able to make psychological sense of more conventional modes as well as of disruptive or inarticulate form. Furthermore, there is no reason why they should not be re-applied to the world of art from which they originally derived.[14] However, they are perhaps best taken as a guide to the 'feel' of a range of typical images, or as a shorthand way of referring to certain fundamental formal idioms, rather than as a systematic map to be followed too closely.

The mention of categories of form and the attempt to introduce some system to enable a better grasp of the multiplicity and variety of aesthetic qualities brings up the issue of how far such qualities can be the object of research, and of what kind of research is most appropriate to them. Whereas such issues are peripheral to both the practice and appreciation of art, art therapy is motivated to confront them both by an internal desire to establish a common frame of discourse and a shared understanding of its practice, and by an externally prompted need to justify its claims to professional effectiveness.

As we saw in Chapter Two, both therapeutic and aesthetic phenomena are only to a limited extent amenable to research in conventionally 'objective' terms: that is, those that are quantifiable, experimentally repeatable and accessible to external observation. Therapeutic boundaries – most obviously those of confidentiality and informed consent – place additional obstacles in the way of such research. However, there are also real problems to do with how far the phenomena being examined may not be destroyed by the very process of their objectification.

Undoubtedly the language that has to be used to explore or 'perform' both the aesthetic qualities of an image and its psychological resonances has to be figurative rather than strictly descriptive (see Chapter Eight). But this does not mean that psychoaesthetic responses are fictitious or subjective: the material aesthetic features of an image act as an anchor or tether to such metaphoric elaborations. The problem is not just one of vocabulary or style: it is more like the difference between a creative process that works with an image, in its imaginative feel or inarticulate form, and one that works on it in terms that are essentially foreign to it. As Sean McNiff (1998) writes: 'Creative arts therapy research has continued in the tradition of psychology while the creative imagination, the essential ingredient of our therapeutic practice, is at best an object of enquiry and rarely the instrument of investigation' (p.17).

Even where 'psychology' in its scientific sense is not invoked, there may still be pressures to privilege the links between the aesthetic features of an artwork and psychodynamic processes. Inevitably this leads into questions about what 'therapy' consists of, and about the differences between therapy in a strictly clinical setting and, for example, the more pervasive notion of 'soul-making' advanced by James Hillman in the previous chapter. As we have seen, art therapy encompasses a wide range of therapeutic interventions, many of which are historically centered on profoundly damaged people for whom such notions might seem a luxury or extravagance. But there are other areas where it does not have to play such a remedial or reparative role.

One of the most interesting places where the worlds of art and of art therapy overlap is in training groups where art therapy students experiment with their own images, or in less therapy-oriented art making workshops for the general public. Here there can be a focus that is 'therapeutic' in the sense of exploring the imaginal or psycho-aesthetic reverberations of images, without necessarily having to invoke group dynamics or individual history. There is an interesting precedent for this in the dream workshops led by James Hillman and Pat Berry a decade ago, where dream images were deliberately worked on in the absence of any biographical context (a similar approach can be found in Ullman and Limmer 1989).

I have found such groups a useful way of experimenting with different ways of talking about or 'figuring out' a picture, without having to depend upon the artist's personal history. In such situations it is possible to refer not only to the artist's intentions, or to his or her actual experience of making the image, but to engage as well in more speculative or imaginative excursions from it. I shall have more to say about the hybrid strategies involved in this in Chapter Eight. Some of these situations would also lend themselves to comparative research into psychoaesthetic phenomena.

Endnotes

1. Freud also developed his own version of a founding myth or speculative paleo-psychology, in works such as 'Totem and Taboo' (1912–13).
2. For a detailed study of this, see Gombrich's essay 'Icones Symbolicae: Philosophies of Symbolism and their bearing on art' (Gombrich 1978).
3. A famous exception is Marion Milne's book-length case study, in which 'Susan's' drawings play an important role (Milner 1969).

4. Jung kept an original series of black notebooks, in which the raw material was detailed: he subsequently worked some of this up in the Red Book whose carefully calligraphed text is illustrated with equally well-crafted pictures.

5. For a complete reproduction of Pollock's drawings and Henderson's admission, see Cernushi 1992.

6. Dr. Navratil set up this facility for a number of his patients in a specially converted annex to the main psychiatric hospital in 1981. Patient artists such as Johann Hauser, Oswald Tschirtner and August Walla thereby acquired considerable fame.

7. For a convenient summary of these early developments see Waller 1991; for more personal accounts see Hill 1945; Lyddiatt 1971; Simon 1992.

8. The Diorama 'Studio Upstairs' in London is a recent recreation of such a studio environment.

9. The first major exhibition of art therapy work was 'The Inner Eye' at the Museum of Modern Art, Oxford in 1978.

10. A somewhat simplistic case for the inherent psychological benefits of art making can be found in Kaplan (2000).

11. I have sometimes wondered whether art therapy could not work almost as well with artworks that were not made by the patient at all.

12. Hans Namuth's famous film of Pollock painting on glass not only helped establish the myth of Abstract Expressionism, but is alleged to have made the artist feel that that he had shown too much (Landau 1985, p.204).

13. I should point out that I made it a rule that everyone, staff or patient, including myself, took part in my art therapy groups in the therapeutic community where I first met this patient.

14. Simon (1992) does make a few attempts at this, for example p.130 where she explores Gainsborough's Mr. & Mrs. Andrews or p.146 where she uses Uccello's Hunt By Night as an example.

Chapter Seven

Towards a New Psychological Aesthetics

... by means of the idea of the unconscious we are able to see into, behind, and below manifest behaviour. But the unconscious is merely a tool for deepening, interiorizing, and subjectifying the apparent. Should we take the unconscious too literally, then it too becomes a husk that constricts the psyche and must be seen through, deliteralized. (Hillman 1975, p.141).

What does 'psychological' mean in this context? So far much of our exploration of the complex relation between the aesthetic and the psychological aspects of painting has revolved largely around terms and assumptions about 'unconscious' aspects of experience that derive from psychoanalysis. This is perhaps not so surprising, since one of the effects of the enormous influence of psychoanalysis has been to encourage the assumption that it alone can account for the nature and working of 'unconscious' mental life, and that as a theory of human nature its dominion extends from the clinical to the cultural. Since painting, both in its imagery and in the spontaneous detail of its facture, involves processes that are not totally under conscious control – and this would surely be one of the reasons for valuing it – then presumably psychoanalysis has a legitimate claim to offer ways of understanding it.

The contest between art and psychoanalysis to link the aesthetic and the psychological

As we saw in the last chapter, in the early phase of psychoanalysis (associated with Freud's 1908 paper on the creative writer, his Leonardo essay of 1910, and his study of Michelangelo in 1914), art could be treated as an innocent or passive object of analysis. Innocent because the artist's collaboration with unconscious processes was under some other aegis, such as inspiration, 'furor' or Saturnine influence (Wittkower 1963, pp.98–107) and passive because artists from pre-Freudian times would have known nothing of psychoanalytic theory and therefore could neither collude with it nor pervert its aims (as, for example, the Surrealists did).

Yet psychoanalysis is far more closely allied to art, not just in its cultural application, but even in its clinical practice, than Freud was able or willing to admit. This is not just because classical analysis deployed a complex and sophisticated network of artistic reference (literature and opera, as well as fine art); but because its hermeneutic strategies have more in common with art and literature than with science (see, for example Fish 1988; Ginzburg 1980).[1] A similar conflict can be seen in Jung's struggle to categorise his personal 'encounter with the unconscious', which involved painting as well as writing, as science rather than as 'art' (Jung 1963).

If to begin with the competition between art and psychoanalysis is one-sided, with a silence on the part of art, then it becomes more open with the diffusion of psychoanalytic theories into culture at large, and with the parallel emergence of more explicitly irrational techniques in art. At first it takes an antagonistic form, with a hostility and suspicion that are mutual. Misgivings on the part of artists are not simply due to the fear many had of their creative work being disqualified or re-worked by psychoanalytic interpretation: it is part of a much larger struggle for the authority to lay claim to psychological exploration and innovation.

Surrealism, with its controversial hi-jacking of both Freudian theories and techniques for what could be called para-therapeutic ends, is only the most obvious and polemical arena in which this contestation takes place. In any case early Surrealist painting uses a paradoxically conservative representational idiom.[2] As we have already seen, certain forms of abstract painting present a more fundamental challenge to psychoanalytic understanding.

Psychological and aesthetic qualities and the figurative inclination of imagination

One considerable line of bias in traditional psychoanalytic perspectives on art is a natural inclination towards the figurative. As we saw in Chapter Three, there is a fundamental collusion between the traditional figurative iconography of art and the kinds of narrative or scenes that are supposed to dominate unconscious phantasy life. While there are ways in which aggressive, disintegrative or erotic impulses can be treated as impersonal, almost abstract forces, the construction of most psychoanalytic interpretations involves scenes, objects or figures and their interaction.

Even where these are not immediately evident, they can still be read into accessory areas of painting, or negative forms. A famous example is the 'vulture' discovered by Oscar Pfister in the drapery of Leonardo's Virgin Mary and St. Anne, but more recently, for example, faces, and even figures, have been found in the 'inarticulate' passages in some of Soutine's paintings (for example Mocquot 1971). This personifying or animating can, of course, be applied to non-representational works of art. Once processes such as condensation or displacement are invoked, figures, faces or scenes can be found in them; but there is always the question as to whether these have been discovered or invented.

This figurative tendency is reinforced by the way in which theories of projective psychology account for the mapping of inner (unconscious) material onto the outer world, a process that is invited by the more suggestive passages of a painting. Such forms of figurative and analogical slippage have a long history in art, from Arcimboldo to Magritte. A well-known example is the 'hallucinatory' visual double entendres in many of Salvador Dali's paintings, which are literally reproductions of this short-circuit between phantasy and reality. Similar visual puns occur in classic 'psychotic art', as Dali and other Surrealist artists knew from Prinzhorn's book (Prinzhorn 1972, originally published 1922). In effect what this amounts to is a deliberate manipulation of Freudian unconscious iconography, so that the privilege of the appearance of external reality over internal, or phantastic, reality is inverted.

As we saw in Chapter Three, this figurative inclination bears witness to a prolonged liaison between the predominant idiom of imagination and ways of 'figuring out' works of art. So powerful is the influence of the psychoanalytic version of this idiom that it amounts to a kind of pictorial lingua franca of the unconscious, and even 'abstract' images can be 'read' according to its light. When passages of inarticulate facture, or informal non-representational paintings, such as De Kooning's, are treated this way, their specific aesthetic features are translated into figurative or narrative forms.

A classic instance of such readings of seemingly non-representational imagery can be found in the series of ten symmetrical ink blots used in the Rorschach Test. The interpretation of these 'abstract' forms is almost always figurative, that is, in terms of 'human, animal or nature responses' (Klopfer and Kelly 1946, p.176).[3] In the next chapter I shall suggest that, instead of facture or inarticulate form of a painting acting simply as a kind of trampoline for such projective leaps, the priority could be reversed, so that figurative animations could be seen as a way of exploring a painting's more abstract, aesthetic features. Of course it could still be argued that such a figurative inclination is natural and inevitable, that human beings are programmed from infancy to interpret ambiguous shapes as figures, above all as faces. Such 'physiognomic perception' does not necessarily have to be 'unconscious' in a psychoanalytic sense.[4] All I am trying to suggest is that there is a danger in tying such figurative readings too tightly either to the workings of physiognomic perception or to an iconography of psychoanalytic motifs.

Critics have argued that the flexibility of figurative projections means that certain informal or suggestive abstract paintings can profit from this tendency in ways that are effectively indiscriminate, unless there is some context beyond the merely 'aesthetic' to anchor our projections. For example, one distinguished art historian writes 'Without some framework against which to test and modify our first impressions, we are left to the tender mercies of our initial projections' (Gombrich 1963b, p.54). The assumption here is that there are no inherent qualities in the material forms of works of art that might induce specific psychological effects, and hence there is the risk that our subjective projections will run amok. In the next chapter we shall see that, providing there is an awareness of its metaphoric or 'as if' character, figurative language can be used as a way of simultaneously exploring and articulating a picture's aesthetic and psychological qualities, and that this is not necessarily an interpretation in iconographic terms.

Another assumption that contributes to the difficulty psychoanalysis has had in coming to grips with the relation between aesthetic and psychological qualities is that it is often assumed that aesthetic features are somehow given to the work of art at a late, if not a final, stage in its making. Supposedly 'deeper' psychological qualities, on the other hand, are assumed to inform the work from the start, and aesthetic factors usually serve to camouflage them. As we have seen, this assumption features both in Freud's theories about art (Chapter One) and in Ehrenzweig's model of the creative process (Chapter Four).

Aesthetic properties and 'communication' in art

These models of the creative process and of the relation between form and content depend, among other things, upon a particular picture of the expressive traffic between the supposed inner world of the artist and, eventually, the spectator and the external support of the artwork. In other words, perceptions, feelings and other mental states of the artist are, consciously or unconsciously, projected or translated into the work of art.[5] This process can then supposedly be gone through in reverse by the spectator, giving access to these features of the artist's inner world. The psychoanalytic 'double whammy', whereby unconscious intentions can be invoked where conscious ones seem to be inadequate, only adds strength to this model. Yet, as we saw in Chapter Two, art does not communicate in quite such a simple way.

For a start, there are obvious epistemological objections to the idea that immaterial mental states or events, such as thoughts, feelings or even 'visions', can be decanted into material and visible form, for example into a painting, without being substantially altered in the process. This is true even for the most illusionistic or hallucinatory-seeming paintings (such as Dali's).[6] If the interplay of aesthetic and psychological is present from the start – indeed from the very first mark – then it is surely more likely that the work shapes the 'feeling' just as much as the artist's 'feeling' shapes the work.

Every creative artist knows the feeling of the work going its own way, coming up with its own sense rather than what we want to put into it, even to the point of seeming to happen of its own accord (this is surely what Picasso meant when he said 'Je ne cherche pas, je trouve' – 'I don't search, I find'). It follows that when the spectator engages with the work, it matters less that he or she retrieves the artist's original intentions, or even that they reconstruct the actual moves the artist made, such as which brushstroke came first, than that they allow the work's material aesthetic qualities to work their own effects upon them.[7] This is not to deny the importance of the ways in which works translate the physical gestures of their making, but simply to avoid making an exclusive identification of them with a work's meaning or psychological effect.

This enables us to shift from the rather programmatic belief that particular colours or forms have psychological effects of a 'stimulus' kind to a recognition that such effects are, even at their most forceful, mediated through our own imaginative and creative responses to them. It is, of course, a truism that the spectator creates the work of art: even Duchamp (1958) said 'It is SPECTATORS who make paintings. Today El Greco is being discovered; the public paints his canvases three hundred years after the creator in question' (p.173, my translation). If the value of works of art consisted largely in their efficiency at communicating states of mind from artist to spectator, even if some of these states were otherwise inexpressible (for example, pre-verbal), it would be a limited one.

Aesthetic qualities and embodiment in paint

This problem is connected with the variety of ways in which the aesthetic properties of a painting can be said to display aspects that are 'embodied', and with the different ways in which such embodiments are beyond the immediate focus of consciousness (without necessarily being 'unconscious' in a psychoanalytic sense). In Chapter Three I sketched a contrast between two different attitudes towards the material facture of paintings: one (represented by Kandinsky) that sought to transcend material conditions and to rise above them into a disembodied 'spiritual' dimension; the other (represented by psychoanalytic theories of anality) that reduced all such ambitions to sublimated versions of basic physical functions.

This opposition is in fact somewhat over-simplified. In the same chapter I also suggested a wider range of 'embodied' responses to aesthetic qualities than that allowed for in psychoanalysis. Nevertheless, we should perhaps start from those aspects that have an obvious and immediate connection with a picture's actual painting. It is evident that aesthetic properties such as pressure or career of line, weight or energy of stroke, and other features of facture carry traces of the artist's movements. Roger Fry, for example, writes about how '... the drawn line is the record of a gesture, and that gesture is modified by the artist's feeling which is thus communicated to us directly' (Fry 1914, pp.33–4).

Other formal properties, such as different orientations of the same form, or contrasts of light and shade, may have an effect upon us which is less directly attributable to actual circumstances of their original making. Some of those Fry lists clearly involve a more speculative or imaginative response on the specta- tor's part: for instance '... we feel [a painted object's] power of resisting movement or communicating its own movement to other bodies, and our imaginative reaction to such an image is governed by our experience of mass in actual life' (Fry 1914). Is there really any clear frontier between this kind of imaginative entering-into the bodily implications of form and more frankly subjective or phantasy responses, that is to say those that for which there is no warrant in the work's actual execution?

I would suggest that this imaginative inhabitation of a painting's facture is accentuated when there are no longer obviously recognisable or reliable figurative clues to depend on. Certain kinds of abstract work, of which De Kooning's is an obvious example, conjure up a 'feel' or resonance that has figurative undertones that are all the more suggestive because there are, apart from the traces of the painting process itself, no specific references to anchor them. Here we are tapping into a kind of liminal area, in between the actual perception of objects, figures or scenes (which have an inevitable interior lining to them) and their recreation in memory, dream and similar imaginative states. In this context, a painting has a peculiar status, in that it is both a real object and at the same time one that calls for an extra and special intensity of imaginative investment.

There are a number of different, although not necessarily mutually exclusive, idioms in which this liminal mixture of psychological and aesthetic qualities can be conveyed. As we shall see in the next chapter, such idioms are metaphoric rather than factual: that is to say, they connect aesthetic features, such as the impetus of brushmarks or the skidding of swathes of colour, with a range of movements or actions that belong to another order than that which presides over a painting's actual creation. Of course, a good deal depends on what 'presiding' means: an artist may not be consciously aware of, or in a position to articulate any of these features, before, during or even after their work. This does not mean, however, that the painting can only have a literal, 'documentary' connection with theses idioms. There is room for a whole range of resonances, and these do not have to be identified with processes that are unconscious in the psychoanalytic sense.

Clearly, the physical process of painting is as much a way of invoking such fantasies as it may be an expression of them. Richard Schiff, writing about De Kooning's paintings of women in the 1960s, explores the intimate (in several senses) relation between the artist's brushmarks and a kind of elementary shorthand for certain parts of the body, to the point where what is involved is '... the drawing or dragging of resistant matter in the mimetic enactment of a physical relationship, *real or imagined*, grasped initially by the eye' (Schiff 1994, p.56, my emphasis).

It is not hard to extend this to the point where fantasies feed into the business of painting and vice versa, so that the painting prompts the painter's feeling just as much as the artist expresses or projects them into the painting. This would be one way of accounting for the fact that several supposedly 'abstract' painters (including Pollock and De Kooning) claimed that their work was always, in some sense, figurative.

Aesthetics, surface and depth

In Chapter Two I indicated some of the problems engendered by splitting psychological life between inner and outer realities, resulting in an internal log-jam of drives, libidinal impulses or affects, and the projections, phantasies or expressions they give rise to, and in a corresponding draining of life and significance from the external world. To avoid some of the contradictions inherent to this model, which is as foundational to psychology as it is to classical psychoanalysis, we may have to challenge the inevitablity of these oppositions between inner and outer, imagination and reality. As we have seen, both Merleau-Ponty and James Hillman have, in their different ways, provided alternatives to them. But we may also have to question the distinctions between surface and depth, manifest and latent level of significance, that underpin psychoanalytic hermeneutics.

It is no coincidence that this other, more radical, alternative is set out in Jean-François Lyotard's (1974) introduction to the French edition of Ehrenzweig's (1967) *The Hidden Order of Art.*[8] Lyotard draws our attention to the representational, even theatrical, framework of psychoanalytic theory, upon which the whole surface-depth distinction depends, with its traffic of projections and introjections. Instead, he proposes that the suspension of boundary between inside and out that happens in art is not a benign illusion or a temporary suspension, but an indication of what is really the case. What art (and here Lyotard includes experimental forms of art such as installation or performance, as well as music or film) gives onto is

> ... a unique libidinal surface without thickness and without limits, not antecedent to the inscriptions that might be traced upon it by the writing of brushmarks, percussion, voice or anything else, but engendered through the operations that metamorphose such affective intensities into colour, sound or phrasing. The artistic body [le corps artiste] is not confined to the artist's body, nor to any body closed in on itself in its supposed volumetric identity (Lyotard 1974, p.20, my translation).

The switch is from processes of translation that operate on a vertical axis, between different levels and almost incompatible modes (such as Freud's primary and secondary processes), to translations on a horizontal or surface axis. It is also from processes that are bound up with representational or symbolic modes to processes that are relatively unbound.

With the former, a whole psychological apparatus is involved, that (re)produces symptoms, dreams, phantasies and art, according to certain prescriptions, which govern both the 'writing' and the 'reading' of signs from a psychoanalytic perspective. With the latter, '... we are dealing with metamorphoses of libidinal energy and with factors regulating these metamorphoses without any privileging of depth being assigned to any one or other of them, everything being similarly surface-bound' (Lyotard 1974, p.15).

Lyotard's concept of a libidinal energy that is mobile and freely displaceable is radically different from the psychoanalytic one, in which libidinal energy is subject first of all to repression (which shifts it to a 'deep', unconscious level), and then to what, in the dream-work, Freud called 'conditions of representability' (that determine its appearance at the surface of consciousness).

At the time Freud was writing it was still possible to bank on the kind of parallels between artistic conventions and unconscious psychic mechanisms that I referred to in Chapter Three; but in a Modernist or post-Modernist culture it is arguable that this can no longer be the case. This is why Lyotard believes that art has a fundamentally disruptive function. It is not just that certain forms of art prove indigestible to this form of assimilation; but that this very model of unconscious psychic operation must be dismantled as a result of encountering them. In this respect he goes several steps further than Ehrenzweig, whose 'inarticulate form' is likewise potentially disturbing of rational order. Lyotard's concept of the 'figure' is, confusingly, quite at odds with conventional notions of representation or figuration: it indicates, on the contrary, whatever is beyond them. This 'beyond', however, is not outside, but within such systems. In language, '… the gamut of gesture that gives rise to depth or representation, far from being signifiable in words, reaches around their margin as their designatory capacity, and is also the cradle of their expressivity, it is their accompaniment, their shadow, and in one sense their end, in another their beginning' (Lyotard 1971, p.14, my translation, adapted).

Just as the figural interferes with the systematic 'discursive' function of language in a variety of ways, so, in more obvious ways, it constitutes the presence of an undefinable, unrepresentable element within painting, however conventional its idiom. Hence 'Art's position is a challenge to the position of discourse. Art's position indicates one of figure's functions, one that is not signified [that is, made explicit], and this function is both around and within discourse' (Lyotad 1971, p.13). The disturbing effect of the figural is a double one: it evokes what is beyond representation, and it produces something like an interference effect within discourse itself.

For Lyotard, art's main effect was to upset or escape the systematic aspects of discourse, for example in the ways in which Cézanne's paintings refuse to be assimilated within the conventions of representation.[9] For him, this had an immediate critical-political implication:

> In the arts, sometimes in painting, sometimes in theatre, music or film … something is always going on that kindles into incandescence what was glowing in the underside of society. […] … artists want … the frustration and repression of libidinal intensities by so-called seriousness, which is only a part of kapitalist paranoia, to be lifted everywhere, and they show how to do this by blowing up the most elementary obstacles, those that oppose desire with the No of so-called reality, the perception of times, spaces, colours, and volumes (Lyotard 1973, pp.19–20, my translation).

Despite Lyotard's detailed exploration of a wide variety of works of art (including paintings by Cézanne, Klee, and Appel), and his demonstration of their individual disruptive figural effects, the fundamental ways in which painting might have these effects are never clearly spelt out.

The only place where some attempt is made to do this is where Lyotard distinguishes between three modes of the figural: the 'figural-image', where elisions or contradictions appear within a figure that still retains some kind of outline or shape; a 'figural-form', where something more like Ehrenzweig's inarticulate form occurs; and a 'figural-matrix' that is something like an invisible source, perhaps equivalent to those aspects of primary process that can only be deduced but never accessed directly (Lyotard 1971, pp.271–9).

However, there are still several more general features of painting that are relevant to Lyotard's approach. One important factor, which does not apply to all painting but is often a prominent feature, is at the level of facture, of the actual kinds of mark made. The connective tissue of a passage of brushwork may be so complicated that one can no longer reliably distinguish one 'mark' from another. This means that a strictly semiotic, or in Lyotard's terms 'discursive', analysis is impossible. Hence Schiff's (1994) description of De Kooning's painting centres on the slipperiness, at once literal and metaphorical, of his marks: 'Woman, rowboat and water – water as both image and constituent medium – everything floats. All is suspended in the changing surface De Kooning sought' (p.60).[10] What is found here in an almost undiluted form, except that there is still a residual 'subject' such as Woman in a Rowboat, can of course also be found in other, more figurative paintings.

It corresponds closely with Ehrenzweig's notion of 'inarticulate form'; but, as we saw in Chapter Five, the latter is something that is perceived at a subliminal level, and is therefore difficult or impossible to articulate at a more conscious, verbal level. In Schiff's dealing with these more fluid, slippery forms, what is at work is something more like shifts from one provisional 'form' to another, a floating attention to different aspects – from small to large-scale and back – of the painting's surface. Such shifts do not have to invoke changes of level, from depth to surface, or the invocation of 'unconscious' meanings, but play over the actual painting's aesthetic features.

In Lyotard's view, the play of energies on or in a painting's surface does not have to be interpreted, or even seen in representational or symbolic terms, with reference to some other level. The parallel might be with the 'free floating attention' of analysis, where the secondary revision of primary process material (such as occurs in the dream-work) is reversed, so that an indefinite range of irrational and unconscious associations is solicited: 'This reversal does not in the least imply the domination of consciousness over the unconscious; it implies a refusal of this domination: what it calls for, is an un-willing, keeping open the space within which the order of discourse and its acts tends to enclose itself' (Lyotard 1971, pp.380–2).

By contrast, in analysis another discourse is eventually introduced in place of, or alongside, this inarticulate or 'unconscious' production, where painting is concerned:

> To understand will no longer be to establish some ultimate libidinal content, even the anxiety provoked by lack … but to determine, in its complexity and its hopeless discretion, the dispositive through which the energy of drives is channelled, blocked, released, exhausted or banked up, in short brought to extremes of intensity… (Lyotard 1974, p.15, my translation).

Even this sounds rather more programmatic than the loose, free-ranging, yet at the same time sensitive and apt language that Schiff and similar writers about art employ. But in Lyotard's own text on Appel (Lyotard 1989) all kinds of strategies – personification, quotation, polemic – and all sorts of discourses – philosophical, biographical, metaphoric – jostle without establishing any priority one over the other. To give just one example from this extraordinary text:

> I quite understand, says colour laughingly,
>
> that before I could be transported,
>
> before I could be metabolised into a sign,
>
> the mind, Appel's mind, had to be tempted
>
> to break through. To be tempted by violent tactics.
>
> It's true that thought finds me irritating,
>
> that, at first, he needed a knife and a spatula
>
> to puncture the coloured appearance of objects
>
> (Lyotard 1989, p.10).

If these kinds of translations are difficult, it is not because they involve negotiating some threshold between conscious and unconscious along the lines laid down by psychoanalysis, but because they involve crossing the border between verbal and pre- or non-verbal domains. Inevitably this entails recourse to a hybrid form of writing, which is neither theory, analysis nor interpretation, let alone description in any straightforward sense. Yet such an 'impure' discourse, with its mixture of modes, may turn out to be the best way of doing justice to the intermingling of aesthetic and psychological qualities in painting. This is what we shall explore in the next chapter.

Endnotes

1. In this context it is significant that Freud felt that Leonardo's art was a more successful form of sublimation than his scientific enquiries (Collins 1997, pp.11–12).
2. It is interesting that Freud, who at first rebuffed the Surrealists' advances, was in the end greatly impressed by Dali's visit in 1938.
3. Independent confirmation of this comes from James Elkins: 'It is significant that it never occurred to Rorschach to ask his patients what they thought of the abstract blots themselves. Instead, they were encouraged to see something else, to 'solve' the 'meaningless' images by creative hallucinations' (Elkins 1999b, p.222).
4. For an informed essay on physiognomic perception see Gombrich 1963b, pp.45–56.
5. For a conscientious philosophical statement of this position see Wollheim 1991.
6. In fact it is likely that much of Dali's work up to 1930 was quite deliberately confected (see Finkelstein 1996).

7. A critic has recently pointed out in relation to Pollock's drip paintings of the early 1950s that '… the kinesthetic sensation evoked by a given mark is often the exact opposite of the movement that actually produced it' (Karmel 1999, p.129).
8. Lyotard's notion of the figural and of how the work of art's aesthetic impact disrupts conventional modes of 'reading' (including those of psychoanalysis) appear first in his *Discours, Figure* (1971) and the contemporaneous 'Freud selon Cézanne', in *Des Dispositifs Pulsionels* (1973).
9. There are close readings of Cézanne in 'Freud selon Cézanne' (1971) and 'La Peinture comme dispositif libidinal' (1972), both collected in Lyotard 1973.
10. Interestingly Schiff has also written an excellent essay on Cézanne (Schiff 1991).

Chapter Eight

Putting Aesthetic and Psychological Qualities into Words

It seems to me that the major modes of interaction with visual images – psychoanalysis, semiotics, gender studies – are also partly forms of repression preventing us from coming to terms with what we are, what kind of writing we are producing, and how we spend our lives. In this arena light reverie, meandering, the gentle deliquescence of ideas, and the allure of half-conscious structures are faithful supports for our chosen condition: they are ineluctable, since they cannot be solved, and they are immobile, in that they cannot be fully apprehended (Elkins 1997, p.xvii).

Elkins is an art historian, writing about the unspoken and unacknowledged aspects of his discipline; about what lies on the edge of, or on the hidden side of, scholarly objectivity. He is telling us that there is a whole range of aesthetic experience that is obscured by the constraints of analytical, critical or academic writing. Putting aesthetic qualities into words has always been acknowledged as something of a problem; but this has significantly intensified since painting began to emancipate itself from verbally explicit iconographic programmes and from the expectation that it should 'tell a story'.[1]

It is not just that nuances of colour, the various pressures of line and the like are difficult to put into words; it is also that the realm of 'feeling' that painting, even in its more figurative forms, connects with is one that is often beyond the reach of language. To quote James Elkins (1999a) again: 'Emotions cannot be excluded from our responses to paint: these thoughts all happen too far from words to be something we can control. Substances occupy the body and the mind, inextricably' (p.98). Furthermore, these 'feelings' are by no means confined to the world of emotions: they include a wide range of psychosomatic inflection.

As we saw in the last chapter, the problems we come across in translating the qualities of paint into words also involve problems to do with trying to relate what is in conscious focus to what lies outside it. In relation to aesthetic properties, inarticulate form is in practice only the most dramatic example of a wide range of features that are not just hard to put into words, but hard to become conscious of in the first place. We encounter comparable difficulties in relation to qualities that are 'psychological' in the broad sense I have tried to give the term. There is also what amounts to an indeterminate area in between the aesthetics and the psychological which is perhaps the most interesting and challenging domain of psychological aesthetics.

We have already seen (in Chapter Three) that according to psychoanalysis, sublimation in painting involves the translation of rudimentary or unconscious ingredients into more symbolic and sophisticated forms. If it also taps into a complex array of bodily phantasy, much of which is pre-verbal or non-verbal, then trying to find some way of suggesting this in words is going to involve strategies that may have to go beyond conventional forms of description. Even without this concept of sublimation, there are still ways in which a creative response to painting requires a willingness to engage in reverie and phantasy, and to explore areas of experience that are irrational or 'unconscious'.

This goes some way towards explaining why there is often a sense of embarrassment or trespass in our attempts to work out what a painting means to us, or even to convey the effect it has on us. We all know how explanations or interpretations that are too dry or analytical seem to kill the life of a painting: as Gregory Corso wrote of certain literary critics:

'They'd amputate the rose to know the rose – and patch it a clumsy detection' (Corso 1960, p.17). Of course it is not a question here of devising a verbal interpretation of a painting that will effectively dismantle the original work of art. Nevertheless, there is something about the sheer visual presence of painting that seems to defy articulation in words, even at a descriptive level, and that has an inhibiting effect.

Perhaps this is why Valéry once said, in relation to Corot, that 'We should apologise for daring to speak about painting'. But what would our appreciation of painting be like if no-one had ever tried to speak or write about it? There would be no culture of response. Writing is both a way of tuning our own response and of helping others to engage with the work. As Valéry himself went on to acknowledge, 'There are important reasons for not keeping silent [since] all the arts live through words. Each work of art demands its response' (quoted Hirsch 1994, p.10).

Of particular interest here is Bachelard's claim that reverie – a mode of poetic phantasy response to literary images – depends upon writing for its elaboration (Bachelard 1969, pp.7–8). For him a merely spoken account is insufficient:

About every image that strikes us, we must ask ourselves: what is the verbal force this image releases within us? How do we pull it loose from the too stable bedrock of our familiar memories? To acquire a feeling for the imaginative role of language, we must patiently seek, in every word, the desire for otherness, for double meaning, for metaphor (Bachelard 1971, p.21).

Of course Bachelard has the advantage of using language to expand on language; but I believe that much of the spirit, if not the actual practice, of his recommendation can be carried over into writing about painting. It has, of course, many similarities with the verbal strategies of James Hillman (see Chapter Five).

Description, interpretation and creative response

The sort of response meant here is something different from situating a painting in its art-historical context, or from explaining its meaning on a symbolic or iconographic level. A creative response not only has to take the risk of exploring psychological areas that may feel subjective; it also has to come to grips with the work's specific aesthetic qualities. To do this we may have to dispense with academic or historical background knowledge, or at least be able to keep it in the wings. But does this mean that we can come up with a response that is purely descriptive?

At first sight it might seem that we could come to grips with the aesthetic features of a work – its colours, its forms, the energies of its composition – through sheer description, without having to introduce any second level of psychological significance, let alone outright interpretation. But we cannot begin to describe anything without some preconceptions about its identity, situation or significance being present, even in the background. In relation to works of art, descriptions are even less innocent, because the experience they both depend on and elaborate is, as we saw in Chapter Two, one that inevitably involves the situation of the person doing the describing. This situation has a subjective aspect, rooted in particular circumstances (the spectator's mood, the local lighting) and it also has more general ones, in the form of cultural, historical or professional influences.

This is not necessarily a disadvantage: if descriptive writing were really to be no more than an account of the work's 'original', literal qualities, then it would run the risk either of being redundant, or of trying to create what would be little more than either a verbal inventory or a literary reproduction of them. A description founded on creative reception must surely entail some element of discovery or invention, as well as close attention to actual specifics. It engenders or suggests a sense, a view or a vision that has not previously been articulated, and indeed could not be, because it owes its very existence to the unpredictable encounter between the spectator and the work of art.

A certain amount of writing about painting nevertheless appears to be largely descriptive. Even at this level there is a spectacular range of response, from the scrupulously attentive to the outright extravagant. We are all familiar with the typical style of art history, in which the material facture of a painting is described as though it were a matter of established fact, carefully tethered to its biographical and historical context. On the other hand, there are examples of 'descriptive' writing that revel in excess, for instance where writers dealing with much-vaunted masterpieces try to match their high aesthetic qualities with 'purple passages' (Pater's excursion on Leonardo's Mona Lisa might serve as an example). In other cases, perhaps where the work is recent and in the course of promotion, there is often a flight into fanciful, inflated or intellectual-ised language, the work itself sometimes seeming to serve merely as a kind of trampoline on which the writer can show off his or her sophistication. This is what has so often given aesthetic appreciation a bad name and made it seem precious and self-indulgent.

However, in relation to established works of art there is often a history of previous encounters which is hard to detach from the work itself. The very notion of 'masterpiece', and the cultural fetishism that goes along with it, can act as a deterrent to creative reception. An obvious example is the work of Van Gogh and the legends that have accumulated around it (Heinich 1996). Spectators who are familiar with this, or some part of it, will have to negotiate their own response to it. In Van Gogh's case, there is the example of Antonin Artaud's essay 'Van Gogh or the Man Suicided by Society', written in two days as a response to an exhibition at the Orangerie in 1947. It is worth quoting a small passage:

> I shall not describe a Van Gogh following Van Gogh, but I shall say that Van Gogh is a painter because he re-members nature, because he has transpired it and made it sweat, he has made it trickle in swathes on his canvases, in something like monumental sheathes of colour, a secular pulverisation of elements, the dreadful elemental pressure of apostrophes, of stripes, of commas, of dashes, of which one can't help believing after him natural features are made up (Artaud 1974, pp.42–3, my translation).

Artaud's essay is one of the most extraordinary, even extreme, instances of creative response to painting, that also re-visions the image of Van Gogh as 'tormented genius' (something with which Artaud himself was identified).

Even without such a history, there is still the sense of an invisible constitu-ency that one addresses in writing about art. It is in this sense that aesthetic responses are 'performed', without necessarily having to have the overtly dramatic quality of Artaud's text. This performance is an internal one, when we rehearse our responses inwardly to a greater or lesser extent, and it is also an external one once the writing of them is involved, even if we do this purportedly for ourselves, somewhat in the way that journals or diaries are never strictly private. In practice the two interact: I may not yet know what I feel until I try to put it into words.

Like the language of feeling, the language of aesthetic response has to re-invent itself continually in order to sound fresh. Even academic writers are sometimes forced to resort to a vocabulary and a style that owes as much to literature as to description or analysis. But, as Michael Baxandall (1991) points out, what would otherwise be a handicap can be turned into a kind of advantage:

> It seems characteristic of the best art critics that they have developed their own ways of meeting the basic absurdity of verbalising about pictures: they have embraced its ostensive and oblique character positively, as it were, as well as bouncing their discourse out of the pseudodescriptive register that carries the worst linear threat (p.73).

In this way recourse to a figurative or metaphoric idiom is not only inevitable but may indeed be desirable.[2]

There can also be circumstances – the approach to a new work, or a new approach to an old work – where the conventional language of art criticism needs to be stretched further. Here, for example, is the critic Adrian Searle writing about Kandinsky's abstract paintings:

> There will be black knobbly staves leaning away from the perpendicular. There will be declamatory curves and hooked arcs which short-circuit between one part of the painting and another. There will be angles. Concentric circles, or near circles, loom and float about, amidst smears and drifts of colour. In places, the paintwork will be flat and clean, in others it will hint at modelling, but it won't model much, or for very long ... All in all, there will be a great deal of activity on the painting's surface, even though the generally hectic composition and incidental rummaging about is alleviated by moments of relaxing white ... There are patches of brightness, like sudden sunlight, and complicated little journeys of serpentine line (Adrian Searle, *The Guardian*, April 13, 1999).

I have selected this because it is a 'fair' account: it rings true as a characterisation, in generic terms, of Kandinsky's pictorial idiom and it doesn't appear to impose any obvious interpretation on it from outside. It is not an objective description, but neither is it aggressively subjective. Nevertheless, the language is resolutely figurative ('declamatory curves', 'incidental rummaging'), indeed at just those points where it feels most appropriate to the painting's abstract forms.

The justice of such descriptions has to do with our sense of 'fit': that is, with the ways in which the similes, analogies and other figures of speech used seem to match the designated properties of the work in question. More than that, they may feel apt insofar as they point to features we had not previously noticed, or that call for just such metaphoric evocation in order to become, in a sense, visible. At the same time, they may suggest various kinds of psychological accompaniment to what would otherwise be a largely formal account. At this stage, such suggestions may be quite diffuse or subtle, or they may closely shadow the work's surface feel. Here, too, response to a painting constitutes a 'performance' of it, somewhat in the way the same musical score may be played in different ways.

This interplay between aesthetic and psychological qualities is often much easier to follow where a painting is more or less representational. The relationship between its subject and the expressive idiom of its facture, between seeing through the painting, whether to scenes, figures or some kind of 'depth', and close attention to its surface, its handling of the material medium or its formal style, is something we are familiar with from both art history and art criticism. But a painting's explicit subject matter is not the only source of its psychological significance: there are also resonances that are much more implicit. Psychoanalytically informed writing about art, at its best, also acknowledges that what is being written about is not simply the outward appearance of the work in question, but the psychological reverberations, often below the threshold of consciousness, that it sets up in the spectator. In this context the philosopher Richard Kuhns (1983) has pointed out the similarity of approach between clinical and cultural situations:

> ... Freud instructs us to enlarge our sensitivity, to become willing to entertain feelings and thoughts that traditionally have been considered inappropriate to the response elicited by works of art. In soliciting our openness, psychoanalytic theory attempts to create parallel circumstances in both artist and audience. Just as the artist creates out of openness to his conscious and unconscious thoughts, so the audience must learn to be responsive with a like availability of psychic content (p.96).

The kind of psychoanalytic criticism that is being invited here is very different from the intellectualised and purely theoretical sophistications of some post-Freudian critics (or indeed artists).

To be faithful to such intermingling of rational and irrational, to the many and various ways of 'knowing' a work of art, entails using a different kind of language from either simple description or outright interpretation. As one psychoanalyst has written: 'The language of aesthetic criticism, should therefore, by means of its own deep-laid metaphor, image a goal of generating new realms of meaning through exploration and discovery, based on passionate congruence between the forms of the inner self and those of the aesthetic object' (Meltzer and Williams 1988, p.181).

It is not necessary to subscribe explicitly to psychoanalytic theory for such resonances between the spectator and the work to occur. As we saw in Chapter Two, all perception involves an interweaving between subject and object; but the experience of looking at a painting intensifies this, especially when it invites us to concentrate on its facture, and writing can enhance this.

Such writing does not always have to be respectful of its subject. For example, Adrian Stokes wrote about Cézanne's Bathers (then a recent acquisition to the National Gallery) in terms that are, for him, quite rough and impolite, and yet accurate in conveying the monumental awkwardness of this painting:

> At first sight these figures could suggest a quorum of naked tramps camped on top of railway carriages as the landscape roars by from left to right ... Beyond the long seal-like woman who regards the depths of the background, the standing, studious, twin-like girls with backs to us lean across towards the trees and clouds as if to be those upright trees (Stokes 1978, p.335).

Later in the same passage Stokes writes about the nude figures feeding on the blue sky:

> The close, clumsy yet heroic flesh sips the sky. These nudes are blue-consuming objects and blue is the only colour almost entirely absent from all the varieties of nourishment. The dissociation invites us to examine them more for their sculptural value, to grasp the monumentality not only of the group but of the knife-sharp, simplified faces without mouths, the alternations between astounding bulk and summary, distorted sharpness... (p.335)

It is particularly interesting that Stokes says that it does not matter if we do not agree with every image that he associates with this picture:

> The emotive arrangements carry a number of such interpretations. Form is a container for a sum of meanings while it is from a concatenation of meanings that form is constructed, meanings that have been translated into terms of spatial significance ... I believe that there is a nexus of meaning that we all

recognise however various our explanations: it is composed from experiences otherwise divergent (p.336).

This notion of some kind of convergence underlying apparently incompatible imaginative constructions of a painting is something to which I shall return.

Aesthetic qualities: facture, style and composition

Even though it is impossible for description to avoid a kind of tacit interpretation, it is still remarkable how seldom descriptive writing stays close to the material aesthetic qualities of a work. This is partly because representational subjects invite figurative responses, whether these are in the form of narrative extensions, animating fantasies or elaborations of feeling or mood, and these can easily distract from attending to the work's aesthetic properties. But it is also because the 'official' language of art history, for example, rarely includes what James Elkins calls 'the language of the studio', talk that centres on the actual, technical and material aspects of the work (Elkins 1997, pp.41–58).

Perhaps it is not surprising, then, that it is hard to find examples of descriptions of specific features, such as colours, lines or brushwork that are not contextually motivated: that is, informed either by the picture's overt subject matter, or else by its historical situation. Fortunately there are also instances of more careful, close attention to the material specifics of painting that are not so inclined. In a recent book, James Elkins (1999a) provides some splendid examples. About a tiny area in a Monet, he writes:

> There is a zoo of marks in this detail that defy any simple description. At the top right is a bizarre boat-shaped trough, made by gouging wet paint with the brush handle, and then pulling it back in perfect symmetry. A pool of Yellow Ochre has been dropped just to its left, and it ran slightly over the lip of the trough before it congealed. To the left of that a streak of Vermilion or Indian Red comes down, leaving an irregular trail over a layer of Cerulean Blue and Lead White ... At the far upper left, some Ochre has just barely skimmed the surface of the canvas, depositing little yellow buds at each intersection of the weave. None of these marks has names: they are all irregular and none is like any other (pp.12–13).

In his writing, Elkins tries to maintain a separation between the 'painterly' and the 'psychological'; but even here he has occasionally to resort to figurative language ('boat-shaped trough', 'buds'), and it is hard to prevent these importations from colouring the general tenor of the text, and smuggling in with them all the figurative and psychological reflexes of animation, personification, narrative and the like. Later we shall see how figurative language that is less tightly tethered to the detail of facture can still do justice to a painting's material aesthetic features.

Closer to a more psychological aesthetics are what could be called stylistic evocations. The most familiar of these are individual ones, where the expressive character or feel of an artist's entire oeuvre is involved. In painting, as in literature, an artist's style can become a kind of signature associated with a complex bundle of images in which both a characteristic facture and a diffuse range of feelings are wrapped up, forming a sort of imaginative shorthand. We talk of Rembrandt-esque gloom or Picasso-esque distortions; even the more 'abstract' idioms of Klee, Miro, Pollock or De Kooning can be similarly invoked. In practice, what is involved here is an idiom which is not simply personal to the artist, but a sort of stylistic trademark that has his or her name attached to it. This relates to the notion touched on in Chapter Five, that there are 'complexes' which are identified by an artist's name, but which are transpersonal. This is why the tracking of artistic influence is sometimes so difficult (see Seigel 1999, p.4).

There are also broader stylistic categories, which refer to movements of periods, which also involve a complex of formal and psychological qualities. These include not only the ones familiar from art history, such as Gothic or Baroque, but also ones exported from other contexts, such as 'psychotic'. The adjectival reach of these terms has become far wider than their original historical or medical context. 'Baroque' can thus refer to works which have a certain kind of extravagant overflow of forms which has only a family resemblance with its seventeenth century prototypes; 'psychotic' to works that display peculiar distortions and repetitions similar to those found, for example, in Prinzhorn's (1972) famous book, without the artist having to be diagnosed as schizophrenic (see Chapter Five).

It is possible to come up with even broader stylistic categories. One is Jung's distinction between 'psychological' and 'visionary' works of art. The original context for this was in literature: 'psychological' refers to what can be understood in terms of familiar human situations (for example, novels dealing with life events), while 'visionary' refers to works where there is an unfamiliar, grotesque or demonic content, more infused with archetypal material (see Jung 1967, pp.87–99).

Jung's concept could plausibly be applied to painting, at least in its various figurative forms: 'psychological' would then correspond to conventional representational or narrative painting, and 'visionary' to works such as Goya's 'Black' paintings, or the painting of Ensor, or Beckmann, for example. I would suggest that the distinction involves not just questions of content, but also accompanying differences in aesthetic form. Rita Simon's (1992) concept of the 'circle of styles' (mentioned in Chapter Six) is another, more sophisticated map of the relation between aesthetic idioms and psychological perspectives.

The point here is simply that all of these stylistic labels refer simultaneously to what I have been calling aesthetic features (such as degree of finish or dislocation of forms) and to a particular psychological 'feel', which may or may not fit into conventional categories of feeling. Stylistic labels can often refer to such psychoaesthetic 'complexes' in a conveniently indicative way, without having to make interpretations or to specify the links between one component and another.

Articulating aesthetics: from figurative to abstract

Some of the difficulties of putting psychoaesthetic qualities into words may, as we have seen, be due to the fact that they are sometimes camouflaged by a painting's recognisable subject matter or content. This is not just a matter of the nature of the works themselves, but of the means whereby we make sense of them. Paintings are not simply illustrations or documentations of imaginative life; they actively shape it, or to be more exact, the ways in which we internalise our response to them does.[3] It often happens that we take in a figurative picture 'naturally', that is to say, passively or unconsciously: we automatically register its ingredients, recognise its subject, and respond to it as we are expected to, without noticing how this has come about.

But in just such instances habits of mind and tacit conventions of imagination are being reinforced. As we saw in Chapter Three, what Freud called 'the conditions of representability' in dreams are merely the tip of an iceberg of figurative habit which has effectively become subliminal or unconscious in our culture. This shows itself not only in the (until recently) prevailing figurative subject matter of painting, but also in both the aesthetic and the psychological language we use to express our response to it. If we use a figurative language that is so closely allied to the representational tradition of art to explore paintings that still subscribe to that tradition, it is hardly surprising that there is a match or fit between the two.[4] But what happens when we come to the more factural (or in Ehrenzweig's term 'inarticulate' see Chapter Four) features of such works?

A classic instance in relation to a detail of a figurative painting occurs in Rilke's (1988) description of Cézanne's portrait Mme Cézanne in a Red Armchair (1877): 'A red, upholstered low armchair has been placed in front of an earthy green wall in which a cobalt-blue pattern ... is very sparingly repeated; the round bulging back curves and slopes forward and down to the

armrests (which are sewn up like the sleeve-stump of an armless man)'
(pp.79–80).

It is true that it is the furniture itself rather than the way it is painted that
attracts this gruesome simile, but similar problems arise when a painter's
handling is being dealt with at close quarters. How is one to describe, for
example, the blissful awkwardness of Bonnard's facture without resorting to
figurative metaphors?

Even when a painting's facture seems so perfectly matched to a recognisable
subject as to be almost imperceptible, as in a naturalistic or illusionistic work, it
may still be worth attending to it. The glassy smoothness of Dali's paintwork,
for example, with its submarine atmosphere, is often allied to a fanatical
attention to detail, realised with an almost microscopic intensity of focus, or to
a delineation of shadow so crisp as to almost seem solid. These effects
contribute to the peculiar aesthetic that is the accompaniment to his hallucinatory technique. On the other hand, still within the domain of 'illusion', a rather
different, dryer, flatter and more remote, facture distinguishes much of
Magritte's painting.[5] What these aesthetic nuances brings out is the subtle
difference between these two artists' styles of illusion: the one focussed on the
virtuosic conjuring up of perverse and intensely realised images, the other
involved in something more like a dry or ironic demonstration of the
conundrums of representational logic.

Of course, there is no reason why the subject and the way it is handled
should not match in other, more 'expressive', contexts: for example, the
weighted, scraped and impastoed facture of Beckmann's triptychs goes hand in
hand with the heavy, world-weary yet monumental nature of his shop-soiled
symbolism. But a painter's 'technique' often tends to get filtered out from
writing about his imagery, and it is still unusual to find texts in which the two
interact.

The aesthetic aspects of a figurative painting may have a more dynamic
relation to its psychological resonance when they differ in some way from the
meanings that could simply be derived from its subject matter. As we saw in
Chapter Six, contradictions between the expected reactions to a picture's
subject matter and the actual effects of its aesthetic features (for example, the
tranquil landscape that feels tense) are an important source of psychological
meaning in art therapy. Psychoanalytic notions of unconscious meaning also
work with this kind of split between surface and depth: the contradiction
between conscious and unconscious intentions is shown, for example, by
anomalies or inconsistencies within the work that can be interpreted as signs of
the artist's conscious intentions being interrupted by unconscious wishes. But

this is only one, rather programmatic, way of reading the relationship between aesthetic and psychological qualities.

Such interactions do not necessarily have to have the inconsistent or contradictory character that psychoanalysis looks for. Soutine's still lives, for example, are certainly not 'still': their brushwork is tumultuous or convulsive, their colour often luridly raw or sickly. It is almost as if there is some final, spasmodic life in the dead creatures, and even the cutlery and cloths next to them twist and bend. The American poet Clayton Eshleman (1998) writes:

> It has always given me pleasure simply to say Soutine's colors,
>
> to reflect on the way his things interpenetrate,
>
> a mahogany table whose cinnabar grain liquifies
>
> around 4 steel-blue, grey and white fish
>
> whose surging immobility is picked up by the rumpled,
>
> knotted ochre cloth (p.87).

One might object that Eshleman takes some poetic licence here, and that this is allowable in poetry but not in more 'academic' styles of writing. But he is simply dramatising what I believe takes place whenever a critic tries to capture something of the aesthetic energies of a painter's work and their psychological reverberations. For example, David Sylvester (1981) wrote about the rhythms in Soutine's landscapes: '... the other experiences the painting [the Landscape at Ceret, 1920 in the Tate] evokes are of a kind that engage our whole bodies: swinging, diving, falling, staggering, skating, climbing, gliding, riding downhill, teetering on a cliff edge' (p.39).[6] This vividly reminds us of the embodied nature of aesthetic response that we explored in Chapter Three.

A good example of the very different ways in which the aesthetic properties of a painting can be played off against its subject matter is afforded by De Kooning's famous series of Woman paintings of the early 1950s. These are direct, full-frontal figures of women with a primitive, almost archaic, character. They are also worked into with vigorous brush-work and excited marks that could be described as painterly incursions into the figures. The women's bodies are carved into by swathes of paint, different parts are dislocated or treated so as to emphasise the analogies between them (such as eyes and breasts); some of the brushstrokes look like graffiti in their raw energy and attack. But a great deal hinges on how this is construed: is its wild energy comparable to the 'attack' of a jazz saxophonist, or is it to be seen as an attack in a more aggressive or sexual sense?

Sidney Geist makes this last identification quite explicit: 'In a gesture that parallels a sexual act, he has vented himself with violence on the canvas which is the body of this woman' (quoted in Prather 1994, p.131). For the psychoanalytic critic Donald Kuspit, these incisive brushstrokes are similarly sexualised, but function at the same time as a distancing device. They '... are deliberate motions in a ceremony of intercourse with woman, more broadly, in a relationship ritualized to keep its emotions under control' (Kuspit 1998, p.282). For Kuspit, and many other critics, the predominant flavour of De Kooning's facture in this context is that of a kind of painterly machismo, if not of a direct, mysogynistic attack on the image of woman.

Of course, it is still possible to maintain that the particular brio in De Kooning's work has something diffusely sexual about it, or that the idiom of his painting, with its brusque, lunging lines, its larded paint and garish colour contrasts, and its sudden fixation on details of eye, mouth, breast or leg amid a welter of indeterminate forms invites a sexualised response. But the question really is: do we have to translate the aesthetic features of these paintings in such a homogeneous fashion? Doesn't this risk narrowing down its range, with its alternation between swipes and blurrings and sharp swerves into definition, between passages that are churned and muddied and sudden epiphanies of pure unadulterated colour, and forcing it through an all too familiar psychological sieve?

To reduce the whole gamut of aesthetic effects here to sexual or aggressive motions seems to be to get stuck either with the iconic – as though these 'attacks', versions of which are found elsewhere in De Kooning's contemporary work, suddenly take on their true meaning in the context of woman's body – or with a translation of painterly gesture into symbolic violence that is too immediate (the same issue arises in connection with Soutine).[7] Perhaps this psychoanalytic inclination, or the sort of moral judgements implied, make it seem that we must choose between these various readings; yet I am going to suggest that this is not always necessary or even desirable.

Because many of the same features of facture appear in De Kooning's abstract paintings, these various descriptions are only partly a response to the subject matter of the Woman series of paintings. Yet, whether they invoke infantile or adult idioms, whether they are more or less metaphoric, they are all tethered to scenarios of unconscious phantasy with the implication that these are the hidden motivations embodied in the facture of De Kooning's work.

The difficulties of writing about aesthetic qualities are exacerbated when we come to abstract works: figurative language, with all its inclination towards animation and narrative seems to contaminate what would otherwise be non-representational. Someone may talk about the 'boot-like red shape at upper left' simply as an expedient way of identifying a specific passage of painting; but such similes have a habit of sticking, or of acting like a kind of after-image. Indeed, given what has already been said about the unavoidability of metaphor in writing about painting, it is hard to imagine how one could write about such works in any other way.

A more dramatic example of figurative animation occurs when Richard Wollheim, writing about these more abstract paintings, describes how 'De Kooning ... crams his pictures with infantile experiences of sucking, touching, biting, excreting, retaining, smearing, sniffing, swallowing, gurgling, stroking, wetting' (quoted Gayford and Wright 1999, p.131)

Although Wollheim points out that these basic bodily processes are contained by the actual near-square format of the canvas, a different, less adult, mode of bodily experience is still invoked, similar to the psychoanalytic range of embodiment touched on in Chapter Three. The various responses to De Kooning's paintings seem to dramatise the idiosyncratic nature of writing about psychoaesthetic qualities. Because each constructs a fairly coherent subtext for the paintings, whether of infantile or adult bodily pleasure, and because these metaphoric interpretations have a psychoanalytic inclination, we might feel that only one can be correct, or else that the contradiction between them cancels them out.

Psychological aesthetics and the scattering of images

Do we have to make choices between different ways of figuring painting out in this way? A scatter of images that are contradictory or incompatible from a logical point of view may still make a different kind of sense, as we saw with Adrian Stokes' text on Cézanne's Bathers ealier in the chapter. As an extreme example, here is part of a poem by Clayton Eshleman about De Kooning's February (1957), in which he has already 'found' a 'Luba jaw':

> The Luba jaw is also the front half of a grand piano,
>
> the rear half of a peacock-blue bison.
>
> This jaw-keyboard-rump is being played or
>
> buggered by a sketchy ape with a feline face.
>
> How curb a dog that's slowly exploding?
>
> Spurting up jaw standing swab
>
> tattered cloak swipe of grey-green mist,
>
> topped by white helmet-shaped woman's hair (Eshleman 1998, p.61).

At first reading it sounds as if the informal marks within the painting are simply being ransacked for extravagant figurative excursions (more extreme, it has to be said, than even the most insistently 'Freudian' interpretation). Eshleman makes no apology and gives no rationale for his confidently subjective imagery; and from one point of view the painting has triggered what are recognisably Eshleman themes. But I think there is also something else going on here.

I don't think that Eshleman is claiming that these figures are 'really' there (that is, at some subliminal or unconscious level); rather, I think he is using them to articulate something about both the material energies and the psychological undertones of De Kooning's paintwork. Each figure dramatises, as it were, a different feature; and their surreal, barely imaginable conjugation cranks up the pitch of the ensemble:

> ... the freedom to belly a grand,
>
> to lay down an X-patch of light-red subliminal
>
> rupture above an erection on stilts −
>
> around an ape-attached-jaw-keyboard-rump
>
> to splash a squarish, splinter-flecked
>
> pool of darker red − not blood red −
>
> dull red coursed by unreadable dark
>
> (Eshleman 1998, p.62).

It would be misleading to see this as an 'interpretation' in any conventional sense: it is, rather, a way of using poetic language to amplify the psychoaesthetic resonance of De Kooning's painting. At the very least he is challenging the reader to follow him, to be as daring in his own response.

This flickering, scattering or playing of images is not a weakness, but a creative asset. Even though one image might seem to contradict another (and Eshleman's crazy hyphening-together confronts us with this), they can still build up to a cumulative effect. The rapid succession of images is not just a hit or miss expedient, or a hedging of interpretative bets, but a kind of chaotic accuracy, in which the jumping and collision of the language both responds to and animates specific features of the painting.

What makes such a language of response seem wild or out of place? For one thing, the tradition of art history tends to inhibit it. The assumption is that certain readings that can be tethered to an historical or biographical context are authorised, while those that are based largely on a response to the aesthetic properties of painting are often left in the limbo of the 'literary' or the 'poetic'. In psychoanalysis, too (as we have seen in Chapter Three), there are pressures to narrow down a work's meaning, and to anchor it in either a supposedly 'instinctual' layer or in forgotten elements of the artist's early life.

Freud's ingenious essays in applying psychoanalytic insights to artists and their work have also set an unfortunate precedent, insofar as their status has gradually shifted from a creative or experimental one (his study of Michelangelo's Moses was originally published anonymously) to one of authority and finality. We have already seen how the search for a hidden unconscious meaning, couched in predominantly iconographic terms, can lead to a work's actual aesthetic properties being disqualified or given a distorted reflection. More important in this context, the freedom of creative response to painting tends to be curtailed by a clinical perspective and by preconceptions about what its psychological content is likely to be.

There are some troublesome questions here, which apply as much to works in an art-critical as in a therapeutic context: who is responsible for the significance of a work of art, the person who created it or psyche in a more general sense? What happens to 'psychological' content at the level of inarticulate form, or on the larger scale of non-representational painting? What sort of language can we use to explore it, and how can we be sure that we are not inventing what we think to discover? If 'art' is being invoked, mightn't this apply not simply to the medium being used, but to the creative perspective with which it is received? What limits are there to this creative reception, or to its elaboration in words?

I cannot pretend to find answers to all these questions; but in relation to them, there are some creative strategies worth exploring which may help us getting stuck in old ruts. The language of Eshleman's poem about De Kooning often turns nouns into verbs or adjectives and stretches or bends it in other ways that wrest it away from its normal representational functions. In a vivid and provocative series of articles about making sense of dream images, James Hillman (1979a) has advanced a number of similar strategies for using language about images that are just as relevant to paintings as they are to dreams. The first is that:

> We can't get at an image at all by sense-perception taken in the usual Aristotelian or empirical view of it. For images are not the same as optical pictures, even if they are like pictures … We do not literally see images or hear metaphors; we perform an operation of insight which is a seeing-through or hearing-into. The sense-words see and hear themselves, become metaphors because, at one and the same time, we are using our senses and also not using them as we may believe we are (p.130).

Of course Hillman is talking here about 'pictures' in relation to acts of imagination, not 'pictures' as actual material works of art. But he is emphasising that the 'laws' of imagination (which is at work not only in our recollections of dreaming but in our inhabitation of paintings) are not necessarily those of external reality.

Hillman's second point is that it is the specifics of an image that need to be attended to, rather than looking for its symbolic meaning according to pre-established formulae (Hillman 1977, pp.65–6). The third point, and the one immediately relevant here, is that the language we use to open up these specifics must be freed from its conventional syntactical functions. For example, nouns should be turned into verbs or adjectives:

> So we reversed the grammar. We freed the noun from its fixity, the arrow from having to be so sharply stuck in its own substantiality. It too can be a qualifier, even present itself in multiple modes – adjective, adverb or verb (to arrow, is arrowing, arrowed). We dissolved the nominative substance (the arrow as naming a thing) into metaphor (the arrow as shifting action and many-faceted qualification) (Hillman 1978, p.166).

Hillman makes a clear statement that these expansive strategies are a way of elaborating the dream's significance, without pinning it down to an interpretation: 'Instead of translating it and supposing it into one or another meaning, I have amplified it by letting it speak in multiple restatements' (Hillman 1978, p.157). This opening out of the image through creative or innovative uses of language is another feature of what I have called the 'performance' involved in the reception of works of art. The word gives a permission for the kind of scattering or playing of imagery that I have just been talking about to be tried out, just as a musical performance can respect the score but still perform a new version of it.

One problem with Hillman's way of working with dreams is that a dream account is, in relation to the original dream, a second-hand version, a translation of the original experience, and hence open to manipulation or revision. Also, there is always the risk that language will take the bit in its teeth and career off; for example in a run of punning connections that depend more on the language being played with than on qualities of the image itself. These 'performances', whether of dream or of artwork, can also sometimes induce a sense of frustration: we seem to be always travelling and never arrive at any destination. Nevertheless, I believe they can be truer to the creative core of aesthetic response than more conclusive modes.

The advantage of comparable work with paintings or drawings is that the work itself is there, a visible image to refer the verbal images to. On the one hand, the aesthetic properties of the work act as a ground for, and a substantial resistance to, the work of phantasy: on the other hand, these 'figurings' can in turn rehearse or articulate aesthetic aspects that would otherwise be beyond words.

What is involved here is much more than just new linguistic devices for describing the aesthetic features of paintings. Eshleman's poem, and Hillman's reworking of language to shift dream accounts out of their conventional narrative tracks, evoke a different sense of the psychological, one that is tapped into by painting just as much as by dreaming or phantasy. Hillman's concept of pathologising as a fundamental idiom of psyche (mentioned in Chapter Five), his vision of an 'underworld' whose laws are different from those of the daylight sensory realm (Hillman 1979a, pp.51–5) and above all his insistence on the necessity for meeting images with images, rather than translating them into concepts (Hillman 1983, p.58) opens up a very different world from that of classical psychoanalysis. Psychological aesthetics must take advantage of these innovations if it is to fulfill its promise.

Endnotes

1. The traditional notion of 'ut pictura poesis' reinforced the link between paintings as visual narratives and the verbal or textual accounts that paralleled them.

2. A very modest account of this is given in 'Figurative language in art history' by Carl Hausman (in Kemal and Gaskell 1991)

3. A striking example of the impact of a new medium on the whole spectrum of imaginative life is the cinema. Films do not simply reproduce many of the effects of dreams, nor do they simply 'enter into' our dreams: they have actually altered the ways in which we dream.

4. This problem is aggravated when psychoanalytic models of unconscious thinking, such as Freud's concept of 'dream-work', with its devices of condensation, displacement and substitution, are used to interpret works of art.

5. This is brought out clearly by the brief 'période vache' in which Magritte deliberately adopted a louche, vulgar facture.

6. This makes an interesting contrast with Adrian Stokes' (1972) description of the effect even of static forms in painting: 'Such immobility, however, often involves a sense of dragging weight, of the curving or swelling of a contour with which we deeply concern ourselves, since we take enormous pleasure, where good drawing makes it profitable, in feeling our way, in crawling, as it were, over a represented volume.' (p.107).

7. See the quotation from Adrian Stokes, p.57.

Conclusion

> What is dying while painting is turning itself into thought isn't painting or art, which are doing well, but aesthetics. Another name is going to have to be found to designate this commentary on art, on painting and on visual art, which seeks out the presuppositions, the undertones, the a priori, but in and through painting, with its means, at the same level as the supporting line and structure. Hegel when he wrote that it is too late for art and that aesthetic's moment has come, has put things back to front... (Lyotard 1991, p.17).

As Lyotard suggests, 'aesthetics' is about far more than a question of what may or may not fit into pre-existing philosophical or psychological theory. The actual aesthetic qualities of painting are often in advance of what theory can analyse or prescribe, and the theory in question may not just be philosophical, but psychological. Such aesthetic features are far more various and unpredictable than those prescribed by traditional aesthetic criteria; and scientific psychologies may also fail to take proper account of them. Furthermore, in the wake of Modernist and post-Modernist thinking, both the nature of aesthetic experience and the kinds of psychological effects that might accompany them have been radically redefined. If only for these reasons, the field of psychological aesthetics is something which could only recently have been established, and much work no doubt has still to be carried out in it.

This book began by charting the rise and fall of the 'aesthetic', tracing its career from its earliest links with truth and beauty, its spectacular climb towards sublimity and transcendence, and its subsequent fall into exaggeration and pretension in fin de siècle decadence. In the course of this history, 'aesthetic' came to refer not just to the philosophical justifications for artistic judgements, but first of all to the qualities necessary for the cultivation of taste, and eventually to the specific characteristics of our experience of art.[1]

At first it seemed possible to establish guidelines for what should count as 'good' aesthetic experience: this was what motivated attempts to draw up conventions of taste. But since the quality of originality in post-Renaissance painting usually involved some stretching or breaking of these standards – whether in finish, choice of subject or colour palette – the yardstick of beauty became something less settled and more turbulent. Indeed, as the expressive aspect of art intensified, the association of the beautiful with harmony, proportion and restraint came to be replaced with more powerful, energetic qualities, brought to a climax in movements such as Expressionism and Futurism.

The emergence of Modernism meant that most, if not all, of the traditional categories on which traditional aesthetic judgements had been based were radically undermined, or effectively demolished. The controversial thrusts of avant-garde art aimed to smash traditional assumptions about harmony, restraint or balance, in both form and content. At the same time other received ideas about art, such as conventional concepts of intentionality or communication, were challenged or refused. In Zurich Dadaism, for example, this contravention of all received ideas was taken to the extreme of asserting that the creation of art is an entirely subjective concern and that there are no accepted criteria for evaluating it: 'An art work is never beautiful, by law, objectively, for everyone' (Tristan Tzara 1963 (1928) p.22, my translation). The Dadaist rejection of any ulterior motive for creating art is like a strange echo of Kant's belief that aesthetic judgement should be disinterested.

The varieties of aesthetic experience

Perhaps a whole book could be written, called 'Varieties of Aesthetic Experience' (echoing William James' *The Varieties of Religious Experience*). In much the same way as James focussed on religious experience, rather than on what theology or religious dogma prescribed, such a book would seek to exemplify the full range of aesthetic experience independent of any moral agenda or philosophical preconceptions. Instead of starting from abstract principles and searching for their more or less successful materialisation in painting of one kind or another, these responses would take as their starting point the actual characteristics of a painting's facture and the specific nature of our response to them, across the whole range.

The revaluing of aesthetic response and its psychological resonances is linked to a recovery of this subjective experience and to a respect for the knowledge that depends upon it. Perhaps it is no accident that the writing that has pushed this frontier forward most forcefully is what would loosely be called 'poetic'. This strain of writing, which has such a respect for feeling and imagination as a part of 'thinking', would include Bachelard and Hillman, for example, as well as poets such as Rilke or Eshleman. One aim of this book has been to sample such writing in order to encourage spectators to be as adventurous as they can manage in their own subjective response to painting without losing sight of its actual aesthetic qualities.

As I argued in Chapter Two, the fact that aesthetic qualities are inherent in the material features of painting does not mean that they are simply 'given', already out there, ready to be registered. It is only when aesthetic response is allowed to take hold, to be 'performed', that it can develop and try to fix these qualities. Language seems to offer the best, or perhaps the only, way of doing this. To continue the photographic metaphor, talking or writing about painting is somewhat like printing from a negative, with all the variation of speeds and papers that are available.

However, although I have sketched out a number of creative strategies for such writing, I do not want to give the impression that aesthetic experience is confined to what can be externally articulated in language. In looking at a painting there is a gradual and surreptitious traffic between inarticulate and unformulated 'events' and some kind of conscious noticing or taking account of them which may not necessarily be verbal.

Some of this articulation happens at a pre-verbal level, or in ways that can only be put into words in a painstaking or indirect way. This may mean that there is an inevitable threshold of difficulty that has to be crossed in accessing such experiences. This would, for example, help explain the complications of some of Ehrenzweig's writing. Indeed, the application of language, or of semiotic analyses based on linguistic notions of the sign, to a painting raises a whole problematic area about what actually constitutes a 'mark', how it might be 'read' in conjunction with other marks, and how these in turn relate to its larger scale elements (such as 'figures').

As James Elkins (1995) has pointed out, 'marks' in drawing or in painting are both semiotic, in that they are meaningful, and non-semiotic, insofar as they do not conform to the criteria for conventional signs. This is precisely why they are so crucial:

> By omitting marks, or herding them into broad categories of 'surface', gesture' or 'handling', art-historical accounts of all sorts make it possible to leap from the recalcitrant, 'meaningless' smears and blotches of a picture to the stories the picture seems to embody. But once it is possible to be historically and ana-lytically specific about graphic marks, it becomes harder to justify that kind of omission and therefore harder to think and write about pictures. It is that difficulty that I am after, whether or not it results in a 'nonsemiotic' position (p.860).

I am, of course, suggesting that it is possible to be specific about such marks without them having to be set in an art-historical context.

The sense of this marginal surplus, this hinterland yet to be explored, or that may be beyond the reach of organised exploration, is surely what also gives some paintings their sense of inexhaustible richness and promise. The relation between this obscure or subliminal experience and language is not necessarily an antagonistic one. I have suggested that language has a creative as well as a documentary role to play in relation to aesthetic experience, just as it does in psychoanalysis. Yet we still seem to lack a literature, let alone an adequate theoretical support, for these aesthetic responses and their psychological repercussions.

In the history of aesthetics, from Plato onwards, aesthetic judgements, and the criteria for making them, were always matters of high seriousness: aesthetic pleasure had to be tethered to moral improvement. Not only has this traditional preoccupation with beauty and truth put a heavy weight on aesthetic response and made it somewhat forbidding, it has also obscured or disqualified much of its true nature. Perhaps it is only recently, with the apparent emancipation of art from many of the religious, moral or political demands previously made on it, that it has become possible to consider a wider range of aesthetic experience.

The responses to these changes in painting's aesthetic effects accentuated their link with interior, psychological dimensions of experience and laid them more open to the charge of being inaccessible or merely subjective. When the 'psychological' began to emerge as a scientific investigation of mental functions, aesthetic experience was at first approached through objective, empirical studies which attempted to put a more quantifiable and average face on these phenomena. But with the advent of psychoanalysis a means was found to explore the more intimate recesses of subjectivity and a whole new 'unconscious' domain could then be linked to aesthetic experience. The pervasive influence of psychoanalytic theories, not only on the contribution of the unconscious to art, but on the psychic realities hidden beneath the surface of civilisation, also brought into question the self-evidence of conventional moral and aesthetic judgements. Or rather, it suggested that they were often determined by less lofty, more primitive motivations than had been previously assumed.

In effect, the widespread cultural adoption of psychoanalytic ideas involved a huge extension of the 'psychological', beyond the realm of the strictly scientific (such as studies of perceptual mechanisms or preferences for colours and shapes) into a hinterland of unconscious experience, where the physiological and the psychological are often hard to separate. This is most obvious in the psychoanalytic concept of 'instincts', but (as we saw in Chapter Three), it also enters into psychoanalytic pictures of the unconscious influence of bodily idioms such as orality and anality.

The danger is that the relatively narrow and instinctually loaded psychoanalytic picture of aesthetic embodiment may seem to disqualify the broader range of ways in which our response to paintings conjures up the body in imagination. From a cultural, rather than a therapeutic, perspective (if the two can really be distinguished), the customary identification of 'psychological' significance with one kind or another of psychoanalytic interpretation has not only eliminated much of the richness and complexity of embodied aesthetic response, but has deterred many people from engaging with it at all.

It is also important to understand that a 'psychological' aesthetics does not have to be divorced by definition from ethical or other human concerns. Rather, such issues are not assigned to it in advance. The fact that they may have to be worked out in individual instances actually puts more responsibility, in every sense of the word, on the viewer.

Aesthetic experience and embodiment

If the 'psychological' has been expanded, so has the meaning of 'aesthetic': the actual material qualities of painting now make an increasingly important contribution to the nature of aesthetic response. While aesthetic theory has often had an abstract or disembodied feel to it, actual aesthetic experiences, particularly in relation to painting, engage with material features which provide them with an external and objective ground. This also gives them a feel that is closer to the physical and the imaginative body than are the abstractions of theory. This more embodied aesthetic response is not dependent upon representation of the human body (as writers like Freedberg insist), but it is also evoked by those material qualities of painting that have to do with the more informal aspects of facture which are most dramatically displayed in Abstract Expressionism.

Such aesthetic qualities are 'embodied' in a number of ways. At the most basic level, a painting embodies the traces of its own making: its washes and brushstrokes suggest the gestures, wild or delicate, originally made by the artist. As we saw in Chapter Three, these traces also evoke a response at a level more governed by phantasy: we recreate not only a version of the painter's body-language, but phantasies about the body in general, its subliminal and imagined life. Psychoanalytic theories give only a partial and retrospective account of these.[2]

For example, in Francis Bacon's paintings of the human figure, impastoed, churned and swiped passages of paint are compressed into the outlined carcass of the body so that there is, almost literally, an elision between gestures of painterly making and bodily motions (internal as well as external). While sexual and excretory functions are certainly, if not flagrantly, exposed, there is also a range of more subtle evocations of the life – and death – of the body. The suavely brushed background and sketched-in spatial settings of Bacon's paintings act as a stage for a kind of metaphoric theatre, in which what is done to or with paint implicitly involves bodies: not just the ones depicted, but those of the spectator and the artist as well.

In this instance, painting both engages with the body explicity, and at the same time suggests, in its material handling of paint, a range of what I have described (in Chapter Three) as subliminal embodied responses. But there are other unconscious responses to the material aesthetic of paintings which point beyond their actual qualities to 'something else' which cannot be described as embodied in the same way.

From the subliminal to the sublime:
aesthetic qualities as indicators of something else

According to almost any school of psychoanalysis, the 'unconscious' is something ungraspable and never directly accessible, only available at one or more remove. Hence it is always possible to believe that it could be related to the aesthetic properties of painting in ways that parallel Platonic concepts of the connection between works of art and the world of ideal forms. Similarly, aesthetic qualities, through the very limitations of their material form, could be seen to point towards an otherwise inaccessible realm. In certain forms of tradi-tional sacred art the divine could only be represented indirectly, by suggestion, or else forms of deliberate anti-naturalism were used in order to distance the image from what it represented (as in certain Russian orthodox icons). Eighteenth century notions of the sublime also conceived of it as something at the edge of the representable. Likewise in certain forms of post-psychoanalytic art the unconscious can only be indicated by secondary symbolic forms, rather than being expressed directly, as opposed to what some modes of 'automatist' form creation seem to promise. The closest we might get to aesthetic qualities which are 'unconscious' in the psychoanalytic sense might be through those informal or 'inarticulate' aesthetic features which are to some extent non- or pre-symbolic. As we saw in Chapter Four, such features would tend to have a disconcerting or confusing psychological effect. In this context it is interesting that a recent book, entitled *Uncontrollable Beauty* reinstates beauty in a new guise:

> The beauty that emerges in these pages has little in common with the monolithic ideals that long dominated aesthetics, only to be all but dropped from the discourse about art in the course of the twentieth century. After being cast out with the same zeal that it was once embraced, beauty is gradually re-emerging without pretense to universalism, as a multi-faceted and ...

uncanny quality that may be present or not in countless forms in any work of art (Schapiro, quoted in Beckley and Schapiro 1998, pp.xxi–xxii).

But the word 'uncanny' is itself elusive, referring perhaps to an experience similar to Rilke's association of beauty with 'dread'. Perhaps this uncanny attribute of beauty is an intensified version of what may be present to a greater or lesser extent in all aesthetic experience.

However, the implied reference here is to Freud's 1909 essay on 'The Uncanny', which deals explicitly with the uncanny as an aesthetic quality. For Freud, what appears so strange or eerie is 'in reality nothing new or foreign, but something familiar and old – established in the mind that has been estranged only by the process of repression'. This is, of course, a typical psychoanalytic account, in which the sublime would feature as a kind of unconscious mirage. But there are other ways in which aesthetic qualities could generate the effect of an indefinable something else.

Sometimes this intention is quite explicit. At its most ambitious, Modernist painting aimed explicitly at a new version of the sublime, for example in the work of Barnett Newman or Mark Rothko. This ambition still continues.[3] But any painting whose aesthetic features have the effect of baffling or blocking the conscious mind might be said to point to an unattainable domain whose characteristics could then be called either 'unconscious' or 'spiritual'. In this way it might seem possible to close the gap between traditional and post-Freudian notions of the aesthetic.

Ehrenzweig's 'inarticulate form' is only the most dramatic and easily demonstrable type of these effects: there is a variety of other modes of what Mark Taylor calls 'disfiguring'. The latter term, reminiscent of Lyotard's 'figural' (Chapter Seven), covers both what eludes or negates the net of figurative likeness and whatever cannot readily be 'figured out': 'In the first place, to disfigure is to de-sign by removing figures, symbols, designs and ornaments. Second, to disfigure is to mar, deform or deface and thus to destroy the beauty of a person or object. Finally, disfiguring is an unfiguring that (impossibly) "figures" the unfigurable' (Taylor 1992, p.8). Even if this may seem to be a somewhat over-inclusive bundle of categories, it nevertheless ties together several of the issues we have been dealing with, and connects them with what could be called strategies for suggesting the unrepresentable. What is entailed here is a kind of via negativa, in which painting indicates this other realm as much through its own inherent absences or faults, as through any sense of fluency surplus surplus (Taylor 1992, pp.86–95).

In other cases similar effects are achieved through a deliberate return to some kind of inarticulate facture that has not been aesthetically 'improved' (in

Ehrenzweig's terms), or one that might be described as deliberately desublimated. In its more extreme forms, such an 'anti-aesthetic' results in a kind of churned-up terrain that provides loopholes for a short-circuit between the material features of facture and a dimension beyond or behind them that could be called at once 'unconscious' and 'spiritual' (for example, Newton 1998). There are interesting echoes here of Marion Milner's ideas about the connections between mystical ecstasy and the baffling of the conscious mind by inarticulate form (see Milner 1987).

Any consideration of the sublime or of something else in connection with painting is bound to involve some conception, however tacit, of the relation between painted marks of forms and what they represent, allude to or suggest. Where aesthetic features of a painting are informal or 'inarticulate', the nature of this connection becomes crucial. This issue is closely allied to the question of the relation between signs and what they signify, or that between symbols and their referents. It also involves the question, raised above, of what constitutes a sign or a mark. Here, too, recent psychoanalytic theory has something to offer, with the idea that there are fundamental differences between two different 'realms', the paternal and the maternal.

Aesthetics and the maternal realm

The paternal is associated with what Lacan called the 'symbolic order': the whole apparatus of symbolism built into culture, of which language is the pre-eminent representative.[4] In this picture there is an inevitable hiatus between what the symbolic order is able to convey, however coherent it may appear, and what lies beyond its reach. For Lacan the operations of the symbolic are 'unconscious' in that we are often unaware of them and take their products for granted. At the same time there is sometimes a sense of distance or loss associated with the hiatus between the symbolic with the comprehension it appears to promise, and what in one way or another disrupts or escapes it. Artistic creation is often thought of as an attempt to bridge this gap, to give a sense of presence or fulfillment where none is actually possible. Some critics have seen Rothko's late paintings, for example, in such tragic terms, reinforced by the artist's own statements and perhaps by his subsequent suicide.

A very different relation is suggested by Julia Kristeva's contrasting notion of the 'maternal realm'. Here the starting point is not the Oedipal moment of separation and distinction carried out under Lacan's 'Law of the Father', but a pre-Oedipal state. This maternal realm depends upon the original intimate relationship with the mother, one whose closeness verges on fusion. Rather confusingly, what Kristeva calls the 'semiotic' is not the domain of distinct signifiers and separate signifeds as analysed by structural linguistics, but a more confused, inchoate realm (which she sometimes calls 'Chora', or 'receptacle') which is pre-verbal and pre-symbolic (Kristeva 1980, pp.133–4).

Aesthetic qualities that would then be associated with this maternal realm would involve features which cannot be straightforwardly 'read' as signs. Kristeva (1989) herself gives an example, in a text on Jackson Pollock:

> Images are suspended, symbols avoided. And nor is the resultant space a symbolic space; it does not depend upon geometry or on geometric forms which derive, as has been said so often, from the articulations of human speech. Pollock's space is infra- and supra-formal, infra- and supra-linguistic, infra- and supra-symbolic (p.39).

For Kristeva, such fluid and informal features dissolve the structures of logic and reason to induce an oceanic, almost mystical state of mind. These ideas, with their spiritual connotations, are very similar to Marion Milner's (1987) thoughts about the links between artistic creativity and mystical surrender, referred to above.

However, it is important to avoid polarising these two realms to the extent that they become incompatible. In both the artistic creation and the creative reception of aesthetic qualities there is a collaboration or interplay between the pre-symbolic and more articulate forms. Linda Coleman (1988) has made a valuable study of the contrasting modes of the father, as representative of mind, logic and reason, and the mother, as associated with the body, the unconscious and reverie. These modes play out on a number of levels: in the clinical practice of analysis, in the biographical influences on key analytic figures (including Freud) and at an historico-cultural level (in the contrast between Enlightenment and Romanticism). The important difference here from Freud's antagonistic picture of primary and secondary processes is that in most creative processes everything depends upon a collaboration between the two.[5]

Inarticulate or unconscious qualities in painting are not the only aesthetic ones

I have so far laid great stress on informal or 'inarticulate' aesthetic properties, but I do not want to leave the reader with the impression that psychological aesthetics is exclusively dependent on these. Of course there are many other aesthetic aspects to painting, with all their various related psychological features. Our culture has its own collective fantasies about creativity, the unconscious and how the interaction between the two is embodied in works of art.

In many ways the association of this inarticulate, unformulated dimension with 'unconscious' creativity, particularly where it is identified with modes of execution that are dramatically spontaneous or automatic, has been misleading. Pollock is the obvious example, but there are many other artists whose creative process has been portrayed in terms of a quasi-automatic fluency.[6] We must try to avoid falling into the trap of identifying exclusively certain kinds of painting, for example those with an obviously informal facture, with such liminal or subliminal effects.

Although the aesthetic effects of such idioms of painting have attracted a good deal of attention, perhaps because they seem so far removed from the deliberation of speech, there are all sorts of other, if less dramatic, ways in which an artist's work escapes his or her control. Many of the most extraordinary aspects of painting are played out under a deceptively modest appearance; for example, in the delicate tonal variations of a Chardin or a Morandi, or the cocktail of local colours in a passage from a Bonnard.[7] Many of these effects appear to be calm and deliberate; but this may be deceptive.

The aim of art is not simply to communicate something that has been already formulated, but to create something unexpected. However skillful or experienced the artist is, he or she is sometimes deliberately skating at the edge of their control. While there are, of course, examples of artworks whose creation has been strictly organised or whose final form is almost completely predictable, one of the reasons why artists create works of art is in order to take themselves by surprise, to discover in the painting something other than a reflection of their own intention. Perhaps this is what Picasso meant when he said 'I am not looking for things: I find them'. Even in paintings with quite explicit programmes or consciously controlled compositions, whether abstract or representational, unpredictable elements can still be found at a more local or detailed level.

In what sense could these be called 'unconscious'? Certainly, even in apparently conventional styles of painting, some spontaneous aspects of facture are, as Ehrenzweig pointed out, beyond conscious control. They may, so to speak, be locally informal even when they have a more formal compositional envelope. In other cases it may be that these more general structural aspects will also be strikingly informal. Soutine's Le Ceret landscapes are good examples of how both levels of informality interact: it is not just the brushwork, but the entire compositional structure that is agitated or convulsive.

Nevertheless, it would be a mistake to identify these informal or inarticulate aspects of painting as purely or simply 'unconscious', even in the general sense in which I have been using the word. What is involved, even in the more spontaneous-seeming modes of creation, is actually a complex collaboration between conscious and unconscious, between the spontaneous and the carefully considered. This is, after all, what is meant by the accumulation of 'experience' in any art form. In his discussion of the psychoanalytic theories of art of Kris and Kaplan, Robert Rogers (1978) writes:

> Discussing shifts in psychic level, they say that when regression goes too far symbolism becomes private, which is not necessarily the case, whereas when control preponderates the resulting work is cold, mechanical, uninspired, which is not necessarily true either. [...] For the 'artist' on a high-wire in a circus, the greater the danger, analogous to involvement, the greater the need for control. This combination of deep involvement with high control offers the greatest satisfaction for the identifying, empathising audience (p.67).

To pitch conscious and unconscious elements, deliberation and spontaneity, or the Apollonian and the Dionysian, against one another results in an exaggeration and a distortion of each (Eshleman and Hillman 1985). Many of the same factors that apply to the creation of a painting also apply to the spectator's creative reception of it. As Jackson Pollock observed, 'The unconscious is a very important side of modern art and I think the unconscious drives do mean a lot in looking at paintings' (quoted Gayford and Wright 1999, p.121). Although Pollock was clearly talking about a psychoanalytic unconscious, his remark can also be understood in the broader sense of the term used here. There is a to and fro traffic in the creative reception of painting between phantasy, imagination and feeling, all of which may derive from a realm that is substantially unconscious, and descriptions, interpretations or analyses that belong to a more conscious or articulate level.

At this stage it could be said that this 'unconscious' does not have to be exclusively situated in either the artist or the spectator. In a sense, it is present in a third party, in the material aesthetics of the painting itself. It is something that is yet to be articulated, and even when someone has managed to suggest something of its qualities in words there will always be a residue which is beyond articulation. Yet this unconscious has an objective and independent status, in that it belongs as much to the properties of the work itself as to the inner worlds of either artist or spectator.

Obviously, some aesthetic effects and their psychological accompaniments are quite deliberate and our response to them is correspondingly conscious. At the humblest level, most of what is covered in instructional manuals on how to paint deals with such effects. But at the level of what Elkins calls 'the language of the studio' more sophisticated connections can be made between quite technical procedures and their psychoaesthetic effects (Elkins 1997, pp.47–50). A painting that is painted with too much control or self-consciousness, however, runs the risk of feeling contrived.

Yet even in paintings where there is a strong element of conventional delib-eration there are features that escape systematic analysis. One obvious example is colour. Writing about Giotto's blue, Julia Kristeva (1977) points out that

> The semiological approach to painting, which sees a language in it, cannot find, among the idiomatic elements identified by linguistics, an equivalent for colour ... it is through colour – colours – that a subject rescues himself from alienation in some code (representational, ideological, symbolic, etc) which he acknowledges as a conscious agent. In the same way, it was through colour that Western painting began to escape the constraints of its narrative and perspectival forms (as shown by Giotto's case), as well as from representation itself (as shown by Cézanne, Matisse, Rothko, Mondrian) (pp.394–5, my translation).

Despite all the technical sophistication of colour charts such as the Ostwald scale, there remains something indescribable about colour in painting, even when it appears in a relatively 'pure' state. Nevertheless, determined attempts were made by Modernist artists such as Mondrian, Kandinsky and Delaunay to find a systematic way of correlating colour relationships with psychological or 'spiritual' states.[8]

For tactical reasons, I have concentrated so far on aesthetic properties which are largely independent of the iconographic or symbolic contexts in which they may be embedded. Yet the example of colour symbolism in Christian religious painting (which might even apply to Giotto's blue) shows that there is often a close and conventional liaison between the two. A certain 'feel' of brushwork can also be the signature of a particular art-historical style, which individual artists may embody in a more dramatic way. El Greco's situation within Mannerism is one example.

Perhaps there are other aesthetic features, such as geometrical proportions, which can be even more readily assimilated by conventional codes. As we saw in Chapter One, these are often the ones chosen as yardsticks in the investiga-tion of aesthetic preference by experimental psychology. While I would not deny the importance of such features, I have chosen to focus on those psychoaesthetic properties that are less amenable to objective measurement precisely because they are both the most difficult to give a systematic account of and those with most to offer in return.

The implications of taking psychological aesthetics seriously

What implications do the phenomena of psychological aesthetics, as I have outlined them, have? They are as large as we care to make them. I have tried to make a case for the crucial importance of what could be called a phenomenology of aesthetic experience, and to show how it is grounded in specific aspects of the material facture of painting. I have argued that all such aesthetic qualities have a psychological lining, whether we are fully aware of it or not, and that these psychological qualities have more to do with phantasy, imagination or poetics than either scientific or psychoanalytic accounts have so far been able to do justice to. They are, nevertheless, worth trying to articulate, and I have suggested some strategies for doing this.

I am not claiming that psychological aesthetics as such is a totally new field: it obviously owes much to other disciplines, such as philosophy, psychology and psychoanalysis. But its importance lies in its attention to the particular qualities of works of art (painting in this case) and our aesthetic responses to them. These responses may refer to, or lean on, many of these theories, but they should not be too strictly prescribed by them.

What might follow from this could, however, entail changes in a number of these disciplines which are involved with art, and some of these changes might be more radical than just alterations of their 'applied' branches. For example, I think there are elements in the nature of psychoaesthetic experience as outlined in this book that confirm the importance of non-dualistic perspectives in philosophy generally. Within the realm of the philosophy of aesthetics, as Lyotard suggests, there might be a shift from overarching theory towards more specific explorations. Nicholas Davey (1999) has pointed out that 'If ... a philosophical aesthetics is to recognise that it is aesthetic, it must respond to the practical question of concrete exemplification (application): that is, with how its ideas can be brought into the particularities of sensuous appearance' (p.24). There might, as Lyotard suggests, come a point at which the accumulation of such instances would bring many previous assumptions of aesthetics into question.

In psychoanalysis there might be changes in how art is dealt with, both as an intra-psychic experience and in terms of its cultural effects. But, as Ehrenzweig's work showed, the implications of giving painting a more active role in these relationships might lead to the radical revision of psychoanalytic theories about the forms of unconscious experience. Other disciplines such as philosophy or psychology might be similarly affected.

On a more modest scale, art criticism and other current forms of writing about art seem already to be moving in the direction of a more psychological aesthetics. This extends into the previously segregated area of art history: I am particularly excited by the thinking of James Elkins in this field. Much work remains to be done towards building up a deposit of particular instances of such applications. But whether they are philosophic, analytical or poetic in style, or an uncategorisable mixture (such as Lyotard's piece from which the epigraph of this chapter is taken), these possibilities will still depend upon the material basis which painting has already established.

Despite all the Modernist emphasis on breaking with tradition, and for all the post-Modernist critiques of essences or originality, there remains an accumulated wealth of painting, a deposit, however fractured or pluralistic, that we can still draw on. At its best, painting can be one of the richest and most complex ways in which the human psyche objectifies itself in the world. As the poet Robert Duncan wrote,

> In works of art, what otherwise had been a passing fancy becomes operative phantasy – the Phantasmagoria, as Goethe called his Helen, or the 'Dream, Vision' of H.D.s Trilogy – to become our history, for our inner history to become a ground of reality, for the gods to flourish, 'stepped out from Velasquez'. The images and utterances that Jung attributes to a Collective Unconscious were all gathered by him, not from the unconscious but from the ground of man's adventures in consciousness, from the works of art (for the telling of a dream belongs, like the telling of a story or the working of an image from stone, to these orders), and are creations of man's conscious life in the community of language. (extracts from 'The Day Book' in Corman 1975, pp.266–7)

Once again, the emphasis is on the crucial role played by language in building up and supporting the constructions of culture, including those surrounding painting.

Yet the 'community' of painting is both through and beyond language. This marginal status presents a lot of difficulties, and is partly responsible for what I have referred to as painting's vulnerability. These difficulties are sometimes aggravated by an artist's aggressively subjective stance, and they are therefore often reacted to in a negative way; but they have a correspondingly positive contribution to make. One of art's attractions is that it constantly finds new ways of pushing forward into a territory that feels quite strange and yet shockingly familiar. A psychological aesthetics provides us with one way of tapping into and elaborating this. My hope is that this book will encourage many people – artists, art lovers, art educators, critics and even therapists – to engage more actively and adventurously with this boundless community of painting.

Endnotes

1. For a preliminary attempt to list the variety of these aesthetic qualities, see Hermeren 1988.
2. A recent and original survey of metaphors in the representation of the body is in Elkins 1999c.
3. See Auping 1987 or Francis 1996.
4. For a useful introduction to this key notion of Lacan's, see MacCannell 1986.

5. Several other writers, including Milner 1987 and Rycroft 1985, have emphasised the cooperative relation between primary and secondary processes in creative work.

6. This is evident in a number of films made of artists at work, including Picasso, Pollock and Karel Appel.

7. This despite Picasso's jibe that Bonnard's colour was 'a pot-pourri of indecision' (quoted in Hyman 1998, where there is a useful summary of the vicissitudes of Bonnard's reputation, pp.211–3).

8. For the most thorough study of this, see Chapter 14 of John Gage's *Colour And Culture* (Gage 1993). Derek Jarman's *Chroma* gives us a less systematic but more poetic set of observations and associations (Jarman 1994).

References

Allen, P. (1992) 'Artist-in-residence: an alternative to "clinification" for art therapists.' *Art Therapy 9*, 1, 22–9.

Allen, P. (1995) *Art is a Way of Knowing*. Boston, MA: Shambhalla.

Artaud, A. (1974) *Oeuvres Completès, Volume XIII*. Paris: Gallimard.

Arnheim, R. (1969) *Visual Thinking*. Los Angeles, CA: University of California Press.

Arp, H. (1951) in R. Motherwell *The Dada Painters and Poets*, p.222.

Auping, M. (1987) 'Beyond the sublime.' In M. Auping (ed) *Abstract Expressionism: The Critical Developments*. New York: Abrams.

Bachelard, G. (1969) *The Poetics of Reverie*. Translated by D. Russell. Boston, MA: Beacon Press.

Bachelard, G. (1971) *On Poetic Imagination and Reverie*. Translated by C. Gaudin. Indianapolis, IN: Bobbs-Merrill.

Bakhtin, M. (1968) *Rabelais and his World*. Translated by H. Iswolsky. London: M.I.T. Press.

Baxandall, M. (1991) 'The language of Art Criticism.' In S. Kemal and I. Gaskell (eds) *The Language of Art History* Cambridge: Cambridge University Press.

Beckley, B. and Schapiro, D. (1998) *Uncontrollable Beauty: Towards A New Aesthetics*. New York: Allworth Press.

Bell, C. (1914) *Art*. London: Chatto and Windus.

Berleant, A. (1990) *The Aesthetics of Environment*.

Bernstein, J. (1992) *The Fate of Art*. London: Polity.

Bollas, C. (1987) *The Shadow of the Object*. London: Free Associations.

Bollas, C. (1993) *Being A Character*. London: Routledge.

Bowie, A. (1990) *Aesthetics and Subjectivity: From Kant to Nietzsche*. Manchester: Manchester University Press.

Bowie, M. (1993) *Psychoanalysis and the Future of Theory*. Oxford: Blackwell.

Cernushi, C. (1992) *Jackson Pollock: The 'Psychoanalytic' Drawings*. London: Duke University Press.

Chapman, H. (2000) 'A view from the boundary: An aesthetic philosopher encounters art and its history.' In J. Swift and J. Swift *Disciplines, Fields and Change in Art Education volume 2 Aesthetics and Art Histories*. Birmingham: ARTicle Press.

Cobb, N. (1992) *Archetypal Imagination*. Hudson: Lindisfarne press.

Coleman, L. (1988) 'The place of the parents in psychoanalytic theory.' *Free Associations 12*, 92–125.

Coles, P. (1990) '"How my mother's embroidered apron unfolds in my life": a study on Arshile Gorky.' *Free Associations 20*, 49–75.

Collins, B. (1997) *Leonardo, Psychoanalysis and Art History*. Evanston: NW: University Press.

Corman, C. (1975) (ed) *The Gist of Origin*. New York: Grossman/Viking.

Corso, G. (1960) *The Happy Birthday of Death*. San Francisco: New Directions.

Corso, G. (1989) *Mindfield*. New York: New Directions.

Crowther, P. (1993) *Art and Embodiment*. Oxford: Oxford University Press.

Damisch, H. (1998) 'Freud with Kant? The enigma of pleasure' In B. Beckley and D. Schapiro (eds) *Uncontrollable Beauty*. New York: Allworth Press.

Davey, N. (1999) 'The hermeneutics of seeing.' In I. Heywood and B. Sandywell (eds) *Interpreting Visual Culture*. London: Routledge.

Dickie, G. (1997) *Introduction To Aesthetics*. Oxford: Oxford University Press.

Didi-Huberman, G. (1996) 'The supposition of the aura: the Now, the Then, and Modernity' In R. Francis. (ed) *Negotiating Rapture*. Chicago: Museum of Contemporary Art.

Dubuffet, J. (1951) *Honneur Aux Valeurs Sauvages*. Paris: La Pierre Volante.

Duchamp, M. (1958) *Marchand Du Sel: Ecrits De Marcel Duchamp*. Paris: Terrain Vague.

Edwards, M. (1989) 'Art, therapy and romanticism.' In T. Dalley and A. Gilroy (eds) *Pictures At An Exhibition*. London: Tavistock/Routledge.

Ehrenzweig, A. (1967) *The Hidden Order Of Art*. London: Weidenfeld and Nicholson.

Ehrenzweig, A. (1975) *The Psychoanalysis Of Artistic Vision and Hearing*. Third edition. London: Sheldon Press.

Eigen, M. (1991) 'Winnicott's area of freedom: the uncompromiseable.' In N. Schwartz-Salant and M. Stein (eds) *Liminality and Transitional Phenomena, Chiron Clinical Series*. Illinois, OH: Chiron Publications.

Elkins, J. (1995) 'Marks, traces, traits, contours, orli, and splendores: nonsemiotic elements in pictures.' *Criticial Enquiry 21*, 822–60.

Elkins, J. (1996) *The Object Stares Back*. New York: Simon and Schuster.

Elkins, J. (1997) *Our Beautiful, Dry and Distant Texts*. Pennsylvania: Pennsylvania State University Press.

Elkins, J. (1999a) *What Painting Is*. London: Routledge.

Elkins, J. (1999b) *Why Are Our Pictures Puzzles?* London: Routledge.

Elkins, J. (1999c) *Pictures of The Body: Pain and Metamorphosis*. Stanford, Stanford University Press.

Eshleman, C. (1998) *From Scratch*. Santa Rosa, CA: Black Sparrow Press.

Eshleman, C. and Hillman, J. (1985) 'A discussion on psychology and poetry (part one).' In *Sulfur 16*. L.A.

Finkelstein, H. (1996) *Salvador Dali's Art and Writing, 1927–47*. Cambridge: Cambridge University Press.

Fish, S. (1988) 'Witholding the missing portion: psychoanalysis and rhetoric.' In F. Meltzer (ed) *The Trial(s) of Psychoanalysis*. Chicago, IL: Chicago University Press.

Foucault, M. (1972) *Histoire De La Folie A L'Age Classique*. Paris: Gallimard.

Francis, R. (1996) (ed) *Negotiating Rapture: The Power of Art to Transform Lives*. Chicago, IL: Museum of Modern Art.

Freedberg, D. (1989) *The Power Of Images*. Chicago, IL: Chicago University Press.

Freud, S. (1907) *Gradiva*

Freud, S. (1908) *The Creative Writer and Daydreaming*. London: Hogarth Press.

Freud, S. (1910) *Leonardo*. London: Hogarth Press.

Freud, S. (1916) *The Uncanny*. London: Hogarth Press.

Gagnebin, M. (1994) *Pour Une Esthetique Psychanalytique*. Paris: P.U.P.

Gage, J. (1993) *Colour and Culture*. London: Thames and Hudson.

Gardner, H. (1973) *The Arts and Human Development*. New York: Wiley.

Gay, V. (1992) *Freud On Sublimation*. New York: State University of New York Press.

Gayford, M. and Wright, K. (1999) *The Penguin Book of Art Writing*. London: Penguin.

Gilman, S. (1988) *Disease and Representation*. Ithaca: Cornell University Press.

Gilroy, A. (1989) 'On occasionally being able to paint.' *Inscape* pp.2–10.

Ginzburg, C. (1980) 'Morelli, Freud and Sherlock Holmes: clues and scientific method.' *History Workshop Journal 9*, 5–36.

Golaszewska, M. (1988) 'Quality, experience and values.' In M. Mitias (ed) *Aesthetic Quality and Aesthetic Experience*. Amsterdam: Eds Rodopi.

Gombrich, E. (1963a) 'On Physiognomic Perception' In *Meditations On A Hobby-Horse*. London: Phaidon.

Gombrich, E. (1963b) 'Expression and communication.' in *Meditations On A Hobby-Horse*. London: Phaidon.

Gombrich, E. (1978) *Symbolic Images*. London: Phaidon.

Haneman, C. (1991) 'Figurative Language in art history' in S. Kemal and I. Gaskell (eds) *The Language of Art History*. Cambridge: Cambridge University Press.

Harrison, T. (1996) *1910: The Emancipation Of Dissonance*. London: University of California Press.

Heinich, N. (1996) *The Glory of Van Gogh*. Translated by P. Browne. New York: Princeton.

Henzell, J. (1994) 'Art as an ally in therapy.' In J. Laing and P. Byrne (eds) *Starting from Scratch*. Edinburgh: Edinburgh University Settlement.

Henzell, J. (1997) 'Art, Madness and anti-psychiatry' In Killick and Schaverien (ed) *Art, Psychotherapy and Psychosis*. London: Routledge.

Hermeren, G. (1988) 'The variety of aesthetic qualities.' In M. Mitias (ed) *Aesthetic Quality and Aesthetic Experience*. Amsterdam: Editions Rodopi.

Hill, A. (1945) *Art Versus Illness*. London: George Allen and Unwin.

Hillman, J. (1975) *Re-Visioning Psychology*. New York: Harper.

Hillman, J. (1977) 'An enquiry into image.' *Spring 1977* pp. 62–89.

Hillman, J. (1978) 'Further notes on images.' *Spring 1978*, pp.152–83.

Hillman, J. (1979a) 'Image sense.' *Spring 1979* pp.130–44.

Hillman, J. (1979b) *The Dream and the Underworld*. New York: Harper.

Hillman, J. (1981) *The Thought Of The Heart*. Eranos Lectures 2. Dallas, TX: Spring Publications.

Hillman, J. (1982) 'Anima mundi: the return of soul to the world.' *Spring 1982*, pp.71–95.

Hillman, J. (1983) *Inter-Views*. New York: Harper.

Hillman, J. (1986) 'Bachelard's Lautréamont: or, psychoanalysis without a patient.' Dallas: Dallas Institute.

Hillman, J. (1998) 'The practice of beauty.' In B. Beckley and D. Schapiro (eds) *Uncontrollable Beauty*. New York: Allworth Press.

Hirsch, E. (1994) (eds) *Transforming Vision: Writers On Art*. Chicago, IL: Art Institute of Chicago.

Hyman, T. (1998) *Bonnard*. London: Thames and Hudson.

James, W. (1902) *The Varieties of Religious Experience*. New York: Modern Library.

Jarman, D. (1994) *Chroma*. London: Century.

Johnson, G.A. (1993) (eds) *The Merleau-Ponty Aesthetics Reader*. Illinois, NW: University Pres.

Jung, C. G. (1959) 'A study in the process of individuation.' *Collected Works*. Translated by R.F.C. Hull. Volume 9. London: Routledge and Kegan Paul.

Jung, C.G. (1960) 'The transcendent function.' *Collected Works*. Translated by R.F.C. Hull. Volume 8. London: Routledge and Kegan Paul.

Jung, C.G. (1963) *Memories, Dreams and Reflections*. Translated by R. and C. Winston. London: Collins and Kegan Paul.

Jung, C.G. (1979) *Word and Image*. (ed. A. Jaffé) New Jersey: Princeton University Press.

Jung, C.G. (1984) *'Picasso': The Spirit In Man, Art and Literature*. London: Ark.

Kafka, F. (1994) *Parables and Paradoxes.* New York: Schocken Books.

Kant, I. (1987) *The Third Critique of Judgement.* Translated by S. Pluhav. Indianapolis, IN: Hackett.

Kaplan, F. (2000) *Art, Science and Art Therapy.* London: Jessica Kingsley Publishers.

Karmel, P. (1999) 'Pollock at work: the films and photographs of Hans Namuth.' In K. Varnedoe (ed) *Jackson Pollock.* London: Tate Gallery.

Kelly, M. (1991) 'Wollheim's "seeing-in" and "representation".' In N. Bryson, M. Holly and K. Moxey (eds) *Visual Theory.* London: Polity Press.

Klein, M. (1986) *The Selected Writings of Melanie Klein.* (ed. J. Mitchell) Harmondsworth: Penguin.

Klopfer, B. and Kelly, D. (1946) *The Rorschach Technique.* New York: World Book Company.

Kristeva, J. (1977) *Polylogue.* Paris: Seuil.

Kristeva, J. (1980) *Desire In Language.* Translated by T. Gova, A. Jardine and L. Mondiez. Oxford: Blackwell.

Kristeva, J. (1989) 'Jackson Pollock's milky way: 1912–56.' Translated by D. Macey. *Journal of Philosophy and the Visual Arts,* 34–40.

Kuhns, R. (1983) *Psychoanalytic Theory of Art.* New York: Columbia University Press.

Kuspit, D. (1993) *The Cult Of The Avant-Garde Artist.* Cambridge: Cambridge University Press.

Kuspit, D. (1998) 'Venus unveiled: De Kooning's melodrama of vulgarity.' In B. Beckley and D. Schapiro (eds) *Uncontrollable Beauty.* New York: Allworth Press.

Landau, E.G. (1985) *Jackson Pollock.* London: Thames and Hudson.

Lanteri-Laura, G. (1984) 'La psychopathologie de l'art comme stratégie de singularité.' In *Art et Fantasme.* Seyssel: Editions du Champ Vallon.

Levens, M. (1995) *Eating Disorders and Magical Control Of The Body.* London: Routledge.

Lichtenberg Ettinger, B. (1999) 'Matrixial gaze and screen: other than phallic, Merleau-Ponty and the late Lacan.' *Journal of the Universities Association for Psychoanalytic Studies 2,* 1, 3–40.

Likierman, M. (1989) 'Clinical significance of aesthetic experience.' *International Review of Psychoanalysis 16,* 133–50.

Lindsay, K. and Vergo, P. (eds) (1982) *Kandinsky: Complete Writings on Art.* Boston, MA: G.K. Hull & Co.

Link, A.M. (1992) 'The social practice of taste in late 18th century Germany.' *Oxford Art Journal 15,* 2, 3–5.

Lopez-Pedraza, R. (1996) *Anselm Kiefer: 'After The Catastrophe'.* London: Thames and Hudson.

Lyddiatt, E.M. (1971) *Spontaneous Painting and Modelling: A Practical Approach to Art Therapy.* London: Constable.

Lyotard, J-F. (1971) *Discours, Figure.* Paris: Klingsiek.

Lyotard, J-F. (1973) *Des Dispositifs Pulsionels.* Paris: Eds 10/18.

Lyotard, J-F. (1974) 'Au delà de la représentation.' Preface to French translation of Ehrenzweig's *The Hidden Order of Art.* Paris: Gallimard.

Lyotard, J-F. (1989) 'Sans Appel.' Translated by D. Macey. *Journal of Philosophy and the Visual Arts,* 8–19.

Lyotard, J-F. (1991) 'Presence'. Translated by M. Hobson and T. Cochran. In S. Kemal and I. Gaskell (eds) *The Language Of Art History.* Cambridge: Cambridge University Press.

MacCannell, J. F. (1986) *Figuring Lacan: Criticism and the Cultural Unconscious.* London: Croom Helm.

Maclagan, D. (1983) 'Freud and the Figurative.' *Inscape.*

Maclagan, D. (1989a) 'Fantasy and the figurative: have they become the univited guests at art therapy's feast?' *The Arts In Psychotherapy 22,* 3, 217–223.

Maclagan, D. (1989b) 'Antonin Artaud and the theatre of pathology.' *Sphinx 2*, 156–73.

Maclagan, D. (1995) 'The Hidden Cost of Outsider Art'. *Raw Vision 12*, 30-7.

Maclagan, D. (1997) 'Has psychotic art become extinct?' In K. Killick and J. Shaverien (eds) *Art, Psychotherapy and Psychosis*. London: Routledge.

Maclagan, D. (1998a) 'Anorexia and the struggle for incarnation.' In D. Sandle (ed) *Diversity and Difference*. London: Free Association Books.

Maclagan, D. (1998b) 'Making for Mother.' In N. Walsh (ed) *Sluicegates of the Mind*. Leeds: Leeds City Art Gallery.

Maclagan, D. (1999) 'The art of madness and the madness of art.' *Raw Vision 27*, 20–28.

Mayer, E.L. (1996) 'Subjectivity and intersubjectivity of clinical facts.' *International Journal of Psychoanalysis 77*, 709–726.

McNiff, S. (1992) *Art As Medicine*. Boston, MA: Shambhalla.

McNiff, S. (1998) *Art Based Research*. London: Jessica Kingsley Publishers.

Merleau-Ponty, M. (1964) *Le Visible et l'Invisible*. Paris: Gallimard.

Meltzer, D. and Williams, M. (1988) *The Apprehension of Beauty*. Strathrow: Clunie Press.

Milner, M. (1969) *The Hands Of The Living God*. London: Hogarth Press.

Milner, M. (1987) *The Suppressed Madness of Sane Men*. London: Tavistock.

Mocquot, M. (1971) 'Les visages de Soutine.' *Expression and Signe 1*, 2.

Moore, T. (1996) *The Re-enchantment Of Everyday Life*. New York: Harper Collins.

Morgan, D. (1996) 'Secret wisdom and self-effacement: the spiritual in art in the modern age' In R. Francis. (ed.) *Negotiating Rapture*. Chicago: Museum of Contemporary Art.

Morgenthaler, W. (1992) *Madness and Art*. Translated by. A. Esman. Nebraska: University of Nebraska Press.

Nietzsche, F. (1956) *The Birth Of Tragedy and The Genealogy Of Morals*. Translated by F. Golffing. New York: Anchor Books.

Newton, S. (1996) 'Painting, Psychoanalysis and Spirituality' (unpublished PhD thesis) Centre for Psychotherapeutic studies, University of Sheffield.

Pickford, R.W. (1972) *Psychology and Visual Aesthetics*. London: Hutchinson.

Pollock, G. (1996) '"The view from Elsewhere": extracts from a semi-public correspondence about the visibility of Desire.' In B. Collins (ed) *Twelve Views Of Manet's 'Bar'*. New York, Princeton University Press.

Prather, M. (1994) *Willem De Kooning: Paintings*. London: Yale University Press.

Prinzhorn, H. (1972) *Artistry Of The Mentally Ill*. Translated by E. Von Brockdorff. New York: Springer.

Rand, H. (1981) *Arshile Gorky: The Implications Of Symbols*. London: Prior.

Rilke, R.M. (1988) *Letters On Cézanne*. Translated by J. Agee. London: Cape.

Robbins, A. (1994) *A Multi-Modal Approach To Creative Art Therapy*. London: Jessica Kingsley Publishers.

Rogers, R. (1978) *Metaphor: A Psychoanalytic View*. Berkeley, CA: University of California Press.

Rycroft, C. (1985) *Psychoanalysis and Beyond*. London: Chatto and Windus.

Sardello, R. (1992) *Facing The World With Soul*. New York: Lindisfarne Press.

Sass, L. (1992) *Madness and Modernism*. Cambridge, MA: Harvard University Press.

Schaverien, J. (1992) *The Revealing Image*. London: Routledge.

Schiff, R. (1991) 'Cézanne's physicality: the politics of touch.' In S. Kemal and I. Gaskell (eds) *The Language Of Art History*. Cambridge: Cambridge University Press.

Schiff, R. (1994) 'Water and lipstick: De Kooning in transition.' In *Willem De Kooning: Paintings*. London: Yale University Press.

Schiller, F. (1954) *On The Aesthetic Education Of Man*. Translated by R. Snell. London: Routledge and Kegan Paul.

Schroder, K. A. (1999) *Egon Schiele: Eros and Passion*. Translated by D. Britt. New York: Prestel.

Segal, H. (1992) *Dream, Phantasy and Art*. London: Tavistock.

Seigel, J. (1999) *Painting After Pollock: Structures of Influence*. London: G B Arts.

Sewell, E. (1971) *The Orphic Voice*. New York: Harper.

Simon, R. (1992) *The Symbolism Of Style*. London: Routledge.

Spector, J. (1972) *The Aesthetics Of Freud*. London: Allen Lane.

Spence, D. (1987) *The Freudian Metaphor*. New York: Norton.

Stokes, A. (1972) *The Image In Form*. London: Penguin.

Stokes, A. (1973) *A Game That Must Be Lost*. Cheadle: Carcanet.

Stokes, A. (1978) *The Collected Writings Of Adrian Stokes, Volume 3*. London: Thames and Hudson.

Sylvester, D. (1981) 'The mysteries of nature within the mysteries of paint.' In E-G. Gruze (ed) *Soutine*. London: Arts Council of Great Britain.

Taylor, M. (1992) *Disfiguring: Art, Architecture, Religion*. Chicago, IL: Chicago University Press.

Thomson, M. (1989) *On Art and Therapy*. London: Virago.

Tuan, Y-F. (1995) *Passing Strange and Wonderful: Aesthetics, Nature and Culture*. New York: Kodanska International.

Tzara, T. (1963) *Sept manifestes Dada*. Paris: Pauvert.

Ullman, M. and Limmer, C. (1989) *The Variety Of Dream Experience*. Guildford: Crucible.

Waller, D. (1991) *Becoming A Profession*. London: Routledge.

Watkins, M. (1981) 'Six approaches to the image in art therapy.' *Spring 1981*, pp.107–27.

West, S. (1993) *Fin De Siècle*. London: Bloomsbury.

Winnicott, D. (1974) *Playing and Reality*. London: Penguin.

Wittkower, R. and Wittkower, M. (1963) *Born Under Saturn*. London: Weidenfeld and Nicholson.

Wollheim, R. (1991) 'Correspondence, projective properties and expression in the arts.' In S. Kemal and I. Gaskell (eds) *The Language Of Art History*. Cambridge: Cambridge University Press.

Worringer, W. (1953) *Abstraction and Empathy*. Translated by M. Bullock. New York: International Universities Press.

Young, R. (1993) 'Psychoanalytic teaching and research: knowing and knowing about.' *Free Associations 3*, 1, 129–37.

Subject Index

Name Index

Printed in the United States
200343BV00001B/325-330/A